ON THE COVER
An upstream view from the middle of Site 1 on the Delaware River near Equinunk, PA.
Photograph courtesy of Jeffrey Cole.

Predicting Flow and Temperature Regimes at Three *Alasmidonta heterodon* Locations in the Delaware River

Technical Report NPS/NER/NRTR—2008/109

Jeffrey C. Cole[1,2], Philip A. Townsend[3], and Keith N. Eshleman[2]

[1]Frostburg State University
Department of Biology
201 Compton Science Center
101 Braddock Road,
Frostburg, MD 21532-2303

[2]UMCES Appalachian Laboratory
301 Braddock Road
Frostburg, MD 21532

[3]University of Wisconsin
Department of Forest Ecology and Management
1630 Linden Drive
Madison, WI 53706

July 2008

U.S. Department of the Interior
National Park Service
Northeast Region
Philadelphia, Pennsylvania

The Northeast Region of the National Park Service (NPS) comprises national parks and related areas in 13 New England and Mid-Atlantic states. The diversity of parks and their resources are reflected in their designations as national parks, seashores, historic sites, recreation areas, military parks, monuments and memorials, and rivers and trails. Biological, physical, and social science research results, natural resource inventory and monitoring data, scientific literature reviews, bibliographies, and proceedings of technical workshops and conferences related to these park units are disseminated through the NPS/NER Technical Report (NRTR) and Natural Resources Report (NRR) series. The reports are a continuation of series with previous acronyms of NPS/PHSO, NPS/MAR, NPS/BSO-RNR, and NPS/NERBOST. Individual parks may also disseminate information through their own report series.

Natural Resources Reports are the designated medium for information on technologies and resource management methods; "how to" resource management papers; proceedings of resource management workshops or conferences; and natural resource program descriptions and resource action plans.

Technical Reports are the designated medium for initially disseminating data and results of biological, physical, and social science research that addresses natural resource management issues; natural resource inventories and monitoring activities; scientific literature reviews; bibliographies; and peer-reviewed proceedings of technical workshops, conferences, or symposia.

Mention of trade names or commercial products does not constitute endorsement or recommendation for use by the National Park Service.

This report was accomplished under Cooperative Agreement 309701200, Task Agreement No. T-3097-03-106 with assistance from the NPS. The statements, findings, conclusions, recommendations, and data in this report are solely those of the author(s), and do not necessarily reflect the views of the U.S. Department of the Interior, National Park Service.

Print copies of reports in these series, produced in limited quantity and only available as long as the supply lasts, or preferably, file copies on CD, may be obtained by sending a request to the address on the back cover. Print copies also may be requested from the NPS Technical Information Center (TIC) by writing to Denver Service Center, PO Box 25287, Denver, CO 80225-0287, sending an email to TIC-Requests@nps.gov, or calling 303-969-2130. A copy charge may be involved. To order this document from TIC, refer to document D-068A.

This report may also be available as a downloadable portable document format file from the Internet at http://www.nps.gov/nero/science/.

Please cite this publication as:

Cole, J. C., P. A. Townsend, and K. N. Eshleman. 2008. Predicting Flow and Temperature Regimes at Three *Alasmidonta heterodon* Locations in the Delaware River. Technical Report NPS/NER/NRTR—2008/109. National Park Service. Philadelphia, PA.

NPS D-068A July 2008

Table of Contents

Figures

Figures (continued)

Tables

Executive Summary

The federally endangered dwarf wedgemussel, *Alasmidonta heterodon*, requires certain habitat conditions for survival, which may include specific temperature and flow regimes. Dewatering caused by chronic drought and increased water demands of the New York City metropolitan area may threaten *A. heterodon* populations in the National Park Service Upper Delaware Scenic and Recreational River (UPDE) by reducing flow levels and increasing water temperatures, particularly during summer months.

In this study, we evaluate discharge and temperature relationships between mainstem Delaware River USGS gages and three known *A. heterodon* locations in order to develop models that will assist managers in preventing detrimental impacts to mussels. We developed discharge and temperature prediction models and depth profiles for each of the three *A. heterodon* sites using established USGS gage and thermal stations. Bathymetry and wetted perimeter data indicate standing water is present at each mussel site during periods of zero within-site discharge. In all three sites it was found that significant benthic habitat would likely be available even under low discharge rates if minimal wetted perimeter (P_{min}) values were maintained. Both discharge prediction and water depth profile models indicate that Site 3 is the most vulnerable of the three sites, as it requires the highest discharge rate (26.3 cms [928.8 cfs]) at the USGS Callicoon gage to maintain both the fully wetted perimeter (P_{full}) and minimal wetted perimeter as well as to prevent occlusion of areas within each site that contain *A. heterodon*. We also developed temperature prediction models for all three sites. Temperature models which included the Kellams Bridge thermal station were most predictive for Sites 1 and 2, while the USGS Callicoon gage was most predictive for Site 3. We observed temperatures at Site 1 to be cooler during periods of extremely warm mainstem temperatures and warmer during periods of extremely cold mainstem temperatures, indicating this site may serve as a thermal refuge for mussels. Simple linear temperature prediction models using established mainstem thermal stations were successful in predicting the site temperatures in Site 2 and 3. As the Site 1 temperature regime did not follow a simple linear trend, a more complex relationship was used for predicting site temperature conditions.

Data from this study indicate that Site 3 is the most vulnerable of the three sites based upon USGS Callicoon gage discharge levels required to: 1) maintain flow into the site, 2) maintain the minimal wetted perimeter, as well as 3) maintain the fully wetted perimeter. The study also showed that if Site 3 is protected then the other two sites would remain protected as indicated by the lower USGS Callicoon gage discharge levels required to maintain similar conditions in Site 1 and Site 2. Depending upon how management objectives relate to *A. heterodon* in the Delaware River, different flow targets would be justified.

This study showed that occlusions occur when discharge at the USGS Callicoon gage is at 12.8 cms (451 cfs). A discharge of 15.8 cms (557 cfs) at the USGS Callicoon gage is required to maintain minimal wetted perimeter (P_{min}) which provides a water refuge within the site in areas where the *A. heterodon* were originally found. The stressed condition of *A. heterodon* within Site 3 during 2002 under low flow conditions (20.8 cms [734.5 cfs]) and warm water temperatures (27.5°C [81.5°F]) at the USGS Callicoon gage, suggests that this P_{min} flow target may not be sufficient to protect the *A. heterodon* when flow levels are low and water temperatures are high. A discharge of 26.3 cms (928 cfs) at the USGS Callicoon gage is required to maintain the fully wetted perimeter (P_{full}) which allows for any shifting in mussel locations within the site that may have occurred since the 2002 Lellis survey. A discharge above 30 cms (1059 cfs) for Site 2 and 27.6 cms (974 cfs) for Site 3 is required to maintain site temperatures within two degrees of mainstem temperatures. However, it is currently unknown whether this temperature difference is physiologically significant to *A. heterodon* under high temperature, low flow conditions. Further physiological and hydrological studies are likely needed to better assess an optimal flow rate to maintain site thermal conditions.

Background

The upper Delaware River supports a diversity of aquatic fauna, including the federally endangered dwarf wedgemussel (*Alasmidonta heterodon*). This mussel species was thought to have been extirpated from the upper Delaware River mainstem until it was identified to occur at three locations in 2000 (Lellis 2001). The upper Delaware mainstem lies almost entirely within the jurisdiction and protection of the Upper Delaware Scenic and Recreational River (UPDE) unit of the National Park Service. Since the construction of the Neversink Reservoir (1953), the Pepacton Reservoir (1954), and the Cannonsville Reservoir (1965) on tributaries of the upper Delaware River and with a Supreme Court Decree of 1954, the river has served as a major supplier of water to the New York City metropolitan area. Consequently, flows in the upper Delaware are often significantly reduced during periods of low runoff, which may potentially impact aquatic habitat and fauna in the river. Existing flow targets for the upper Delaware are now under revision. In this study, we evaluate the effects of mainstem flow and corresponding water temperatures on conditions at known *A. heterodon* locations. We also assess potential flow-related impacts to mussels in the upper Delaware River.

Under the 1954 Supreme Court Decree, the city of New York must release enough water from reservoirs in the upper Delaware River to maintain a flow of 1,750 cfs at the USGS Montague gage (#01438500) at river mile 246.8. This gage is located 25.5 km (15.8 mi) below the southern terminus of UPDE. During the past 30 years, the city has met minimum flow targets mostly through releases of water from the Cannonsville Reservoir on the West Branch located upstream of known *A. heterodon* locations. Recent proposals for future water management include revised reservoir releases from impoundments on the Lackawaxen and Mongaup rivers, located downstream of *A. heterodon* locations. Such releases, without flow contributions from upstream reservoirs, could alone achieve the flow targets at the Montague gage (Serio 2002) (Figure 1). If the minimum flow target was met solely through releases from the Lackawaxen and Mongaup rivers, and water were continually withdrawn from the Pepacton and Cannonsville reservoirs on the East and West Branches of the Delaware, a total of 116.6 km (72.5 mi) of the Delaware River within UPDE could be significantly dewatered. This could potentially endanger riverine habitat and aquatic organisms in the upper Delaware River mainstem. Such conditions could put *A. heterodon* at risk in particular, as two of the three known *A. heterodon* locations are found in side channels and may become occluded during low flow conditions. Due to increasing water needs of the New York City metropolitan area, which draws water from these reservoirs on the East and West Branches, river managers may institute an increase in withdrawals from these reservoirs. The upper Delaware River mainstem and UPDE, contained entirely within the 115.8-km (72-mi) stretch between Hancock and Port Jervis, NY, may be severely impacted by such flow reductions, particularly if minimum flow requirements at Montague are sustained largely through releases from the Mongaup and Lackawaxen rivers rather than releases from the East and West Branches.

Surveys of freshwater mussels in UPDE have revealed three locations containing a disperse population of the federally endangered *A. heterodon* (Lellis 2001). We observed that this mussel species in the Delaware River basin generally occurs in low gradient areas where water is less than 1 m (3.3 ft) in depth, and is often found near islands. As a consequence, areas containing

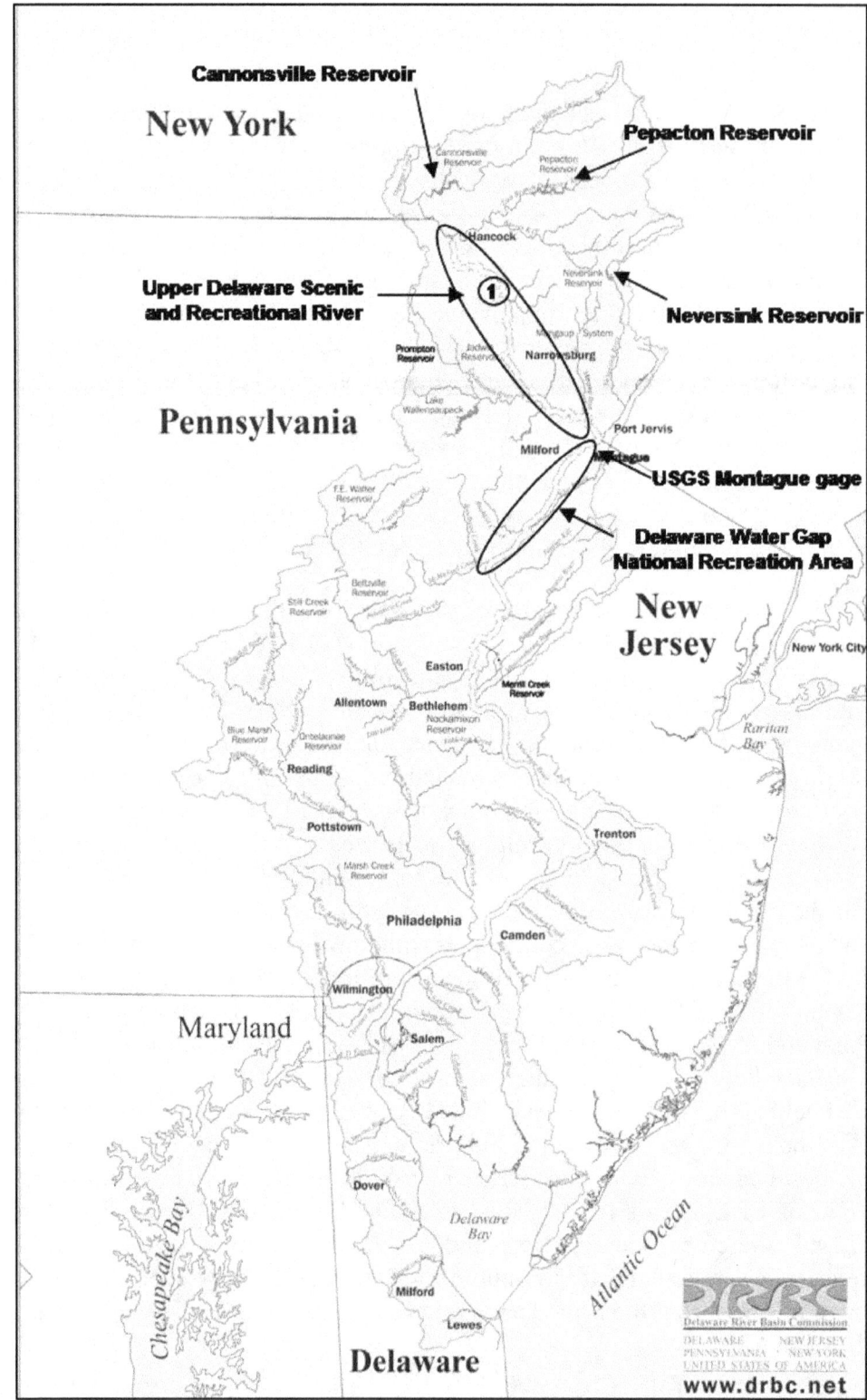

Figure 1. Map of the Delaware River drainage area showing all major tributaries, reservoirs, national parks, and some reference cities. (Source: Delaware River Basin Commission website: http://www.state.nj.us/drbc/edweb/maps.htm.)

A. heterodon could potentially be among the first to dewater if minimum river flow were reduced below the existing target. This could potentially exclude mussels from critical habitat and expose them to hyperthermia, anoxia, and/or dehydration during summer droughts, and freezing and upheaval during winter droughts. Dewatering during any season also exposes mussels to increased predation and may decouple mussel from their fish host (Morales, Weber et al. 2006). The objectives of this study are to:

1) use a predictive model to determine the relationship between stage and discharge at *A. heterodon* sites and data from USGS gage stations;

2) determine on-location relationships between stage and wetted perimeter so that a predictive model could be used to estimate site conditions based on data recorded at USGS gage stations; and

3) determine the relationships between established thermal stations and temperature at *A. heterodon* sites as well as determine the relationship between on-location temperature profiles and flow conditions, such that a predictive model can be used to estimate temperature conditions at the *A. heterodon* sites based on data from the established thermal stations.

This project was completed to fulfill PMIS (#89044) which will help UPDE resource managers to make informed recommendations to other management agencies on water flow requirements conducive to the survival of *A. heterodon* mussels in the upper Delaware River. This project also supports several specific recovery tasks listed in the Dwarf Wedge Mussel Recovery Plan (USFWS 1993). These include Task 1.11: Conduct studies of species' distribution and status; Task 1.2: Identify essential habitat and key areas in need of protection; and Task 4.2: Characterize the species' habitat requirements for all life history stages.

Methods

Site Selection

The three study sites in this project were locations in the upper Delaware River that were determined in 2000 to contain subpopulations of *A. heterodon* (Lellis 2001, Figure 2). To define the boundaries of each site, we buffered the areas of the known *A. heterodon* upriver and downriver approximately 400 m (1,312 ft). This ensured that we assessed known locations of *A. heterodon* populations as well as any minor shifts in mussel distribution that may have occurred within each site since the original 2000 survey. Surrogate sites were designated for the temperature analysis to compare water temperatures at mussel locations with those in adjacent channels or reaches of the river unoccupied by *A. heterodon*.

Site 1 included the channel on the Pennsylvania side of the island near river mile 323 upstream of Equinunk, PA (Figure 3). This was the northernmost sample site and was 1,696 m (5,564 ft) in length. The boundaries were defined by the Pennsylvania bank on one side and by the bank of the island system on the other. The site was subdivided into cross- sectional transects every 100 m (328 ft) starting at the upstream boundary. There were a total of 17 transects in this site. Starting at the upstream boundary of the site, each transect was assigned an identification letter and number starting with F0 at the uppermost transect and continuing south at intervals through F1696 based on distance from the upstream boundary of the site. A staff gage was installed at transect F977. A concrete benchmark was installed near transect F977 and metal headpins were installed at the origin of each transect to be used as reference points for measurements taken during the study. The surrogate site for temperature analysis was designated as the channel on the New York side of this island.

Site 2 was located 18 km (11.2 mi) downstream from Site 1 and was 697 m (2,286.7 ft) in length (Table 1, Figure 4). For Site 2, site boundaries were not natural boundaries determined by island formations; rather we delineated the site to include an area along the Pennsylvania shoreline known to contain *A. heterodon*. At this site, *A. heterodon* have been observed at relatively shallow depths of moderate flow velocity, and are rarely found more than 34 m (111.5 ft) from the shoreline. For these reasons, we defined the boundaries to be the Pennsylvania bank on one side and a parallel line 34 m (111.5 ft) from this bank as the other side. The upstream boundary of this site was located near the point where Cooley Creek enters the Delaware River, upstream of the area where *A. heterodon* have been observed. The downstream boundary was located near a natural constriction point, downstream from the *A. heterodon* locations. The site was defined to extend 34 m (111.5 ft) from the western (PA) shore, based on the maximum distance *A. heterodon* have been observed from the bank (U.S. Geological Survey, W. Lellis, Supervisory Fish Biologist, pers. comm., January 2004). Site 2 was subdivided into 8 transects in the same manner as Site 1 and metal headpins were installed at the origin of each transect for referencing purposes. Transects were designated from H0 at the upstream boundary to H697 at the downstream boundary. The staff gage and benchmark were installed at transect H297. The surrogate site for Site 2 was delineated as the New York bank opposite the *A. heterodon* location which was also unoccupied by *A. heterodon*.

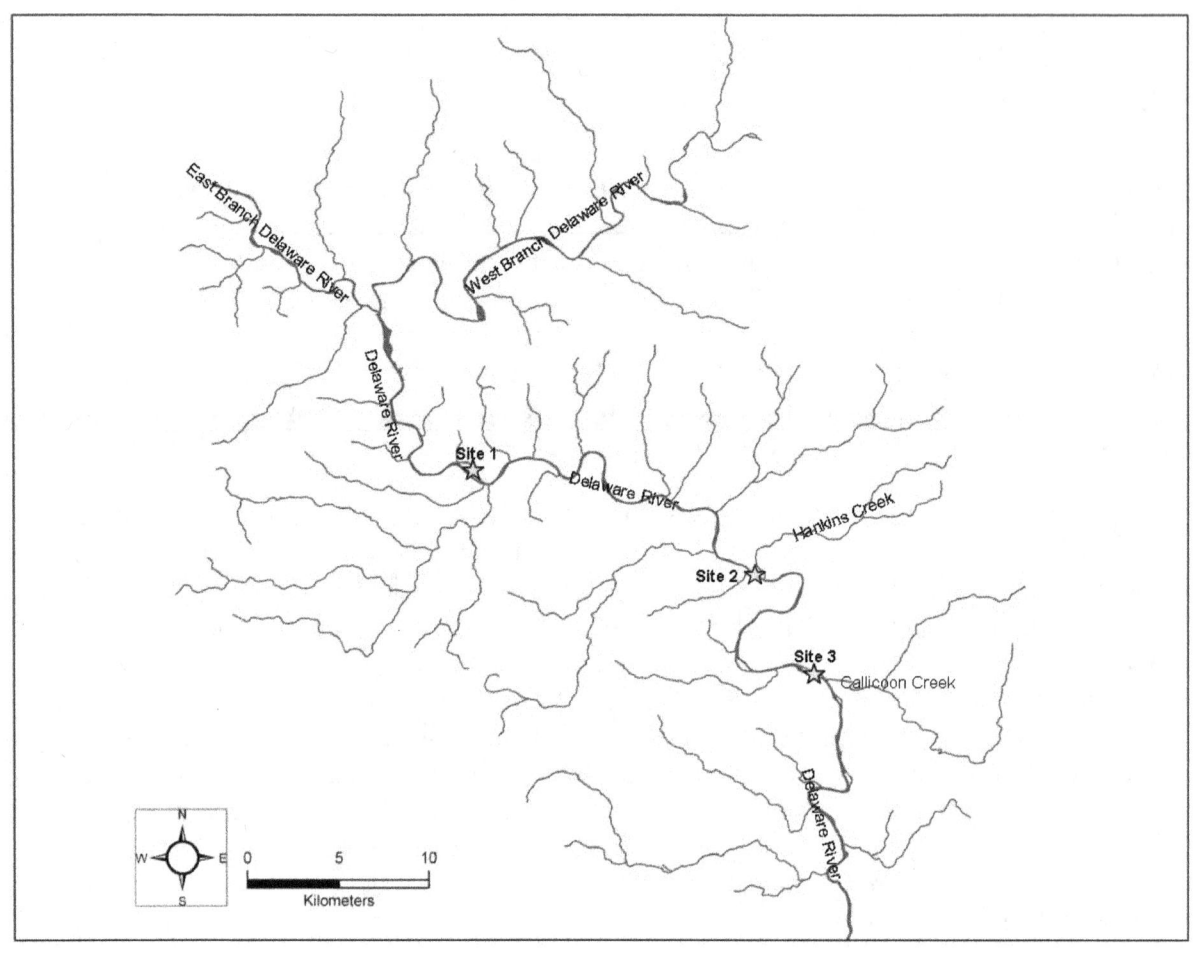

Figure 2. Map of the upper Delaware River showing the locations of Sites 1, 2, and 3.

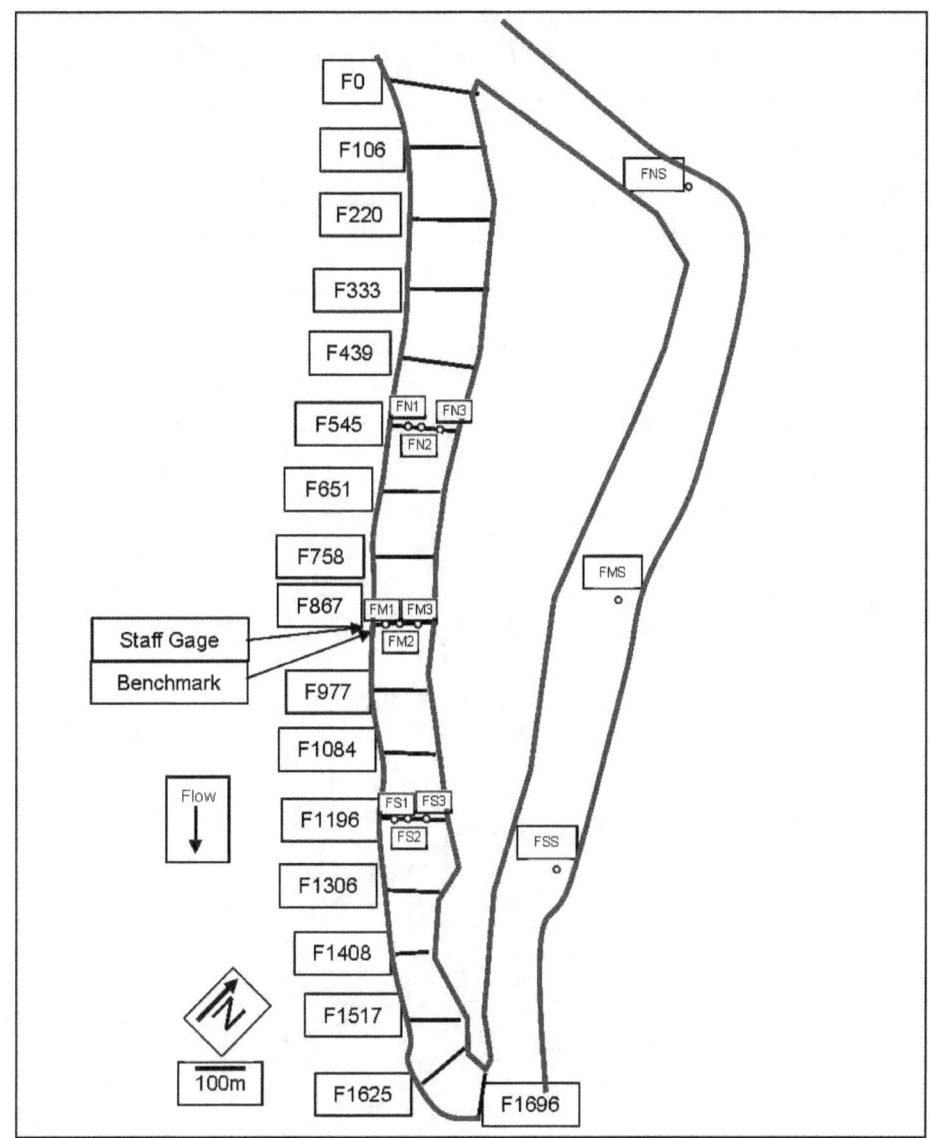

Figure 3. Site map of Site 1, showing transect layout, transect name, and staff gage and benchmark locations. Yellow dots represent temperature data logger locations and are labeled with identification name.

Table 1. River distances (km) between points of interest within the Delaware River. The USGS Fishs Eddy and USGS Hale Eddy gages are located upstream of the *Alasmidonta heterodon* sites, while the USGS Callicoon gage is downstream.

Site	USGS Fishs Eddy gage	USGS Hale Eddy gage	Site 1	Site 2	Site 3	USGS Callicoon gage
Site 1	30.0	27.7	-	18.0	29.0	30.2
Site 2	48.0	45.7	18.0	-	11.0	12.2
Site 3	59.0	56.7	29.0	11.0	-	1.2

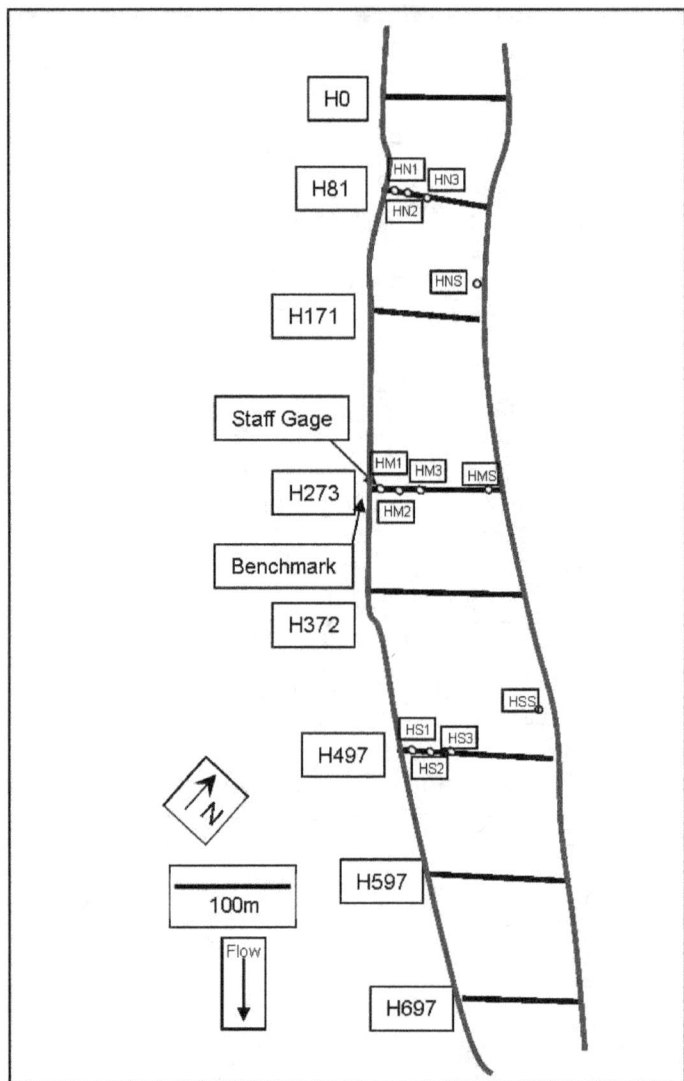

Figure 4. Site map of Site 2, showing transect layout, transect name, and staff gage and benchmark locations. Yellow dots represent temperature data logger locations and are labeled with identification name.

Site 3 was located furthest downstream. This site was 1,155 m (3,789 ft) in length and included the entire channel along the Pennsylvania side of an island chain near Callicoon, NY, at river mile 305 (Figure 5). The side boundaries for Site 3 were defined by the Pennsylvania bank on one side and by the bank of the island system on the other side. The upstream boundary of this site was at the top of the island chain and a bridge was used as the downstream boundary marker. Site 3 was subdivided into 14 transects, ranging from C0 at the upstream boundary to C1155 at the downstream boundary in the same manner as Sites 1 and 2. As with the other two sites, metal headpins were installed along the Pennsylvania bank at the origin of each transect. The staff gage was installed at transect C752 and a concrete benchmark was installed near transect C752. The surrogate temperature site for Site 3 was designated as the channel on the New York side of this island system.

Field Measurements

Bathymetry measurements, rating curve data, and temperature data were first collected during the summer of 2004. A series of flood events occurred during fall of 2004 and one severe flood occurred during April 2005 (40–80 year recurrence interval). These events may have changed river morphology at the three study sites, so we collected a second set of data during 2005. All data collected during 2004 and 2005 were then compared to ensure that our models accurately reflected any changes that might have occurred within the sites as a result of these flood events.

Rating Curve Data

Data were collected to develop partial river discharge rating curves at all three sites over a range of stage values during 2004 and 2005. Partial river discharge only included flow through the mussel sites. First, a single transect near known *A. heterodon* within the site was designated to represent the site, and a corresponding staff gage was installed along that transect. We performed nine rating events for both Site 1 and Site 2 ranging in stage at Site 1 from 0.41–0.83 m (1.35–2.76 ft) and at Site 2 from 0.44–1.06 m (1.44–3.48 ft). For a single rating event, we measured water depth (m) and velocity (m/s) at 20% and 80% of the depth across the staff gage transect at each mussel site at a specific discharge level. We conducted 11 rating events for Site 3, ranging in stage values from 0.46–1.04 m (1.51–3.41 ft). Rating data were collected at 3-m (9.84-ft) intervals across the staff gage transect with a portable flow meter (FLO-MATE Model 2000, Marsh-McBirney, Inc., Frederick, MD). We collected data primarily during low flow events as low flows are hypothesized to pose a significant threat to *A. heterodon*. Water depths at the staff gage were also recorded periodically at each site throughout the 2004 and 2005 survey seasons. Rating data and staff gage measurements were later used to calculate partial river (site) discharge and to develop discharge prediction models. A total of 19 additional gage readings were incorporated into Site 1 prediction models, 109 for Site 2, and 20 for Site 3.

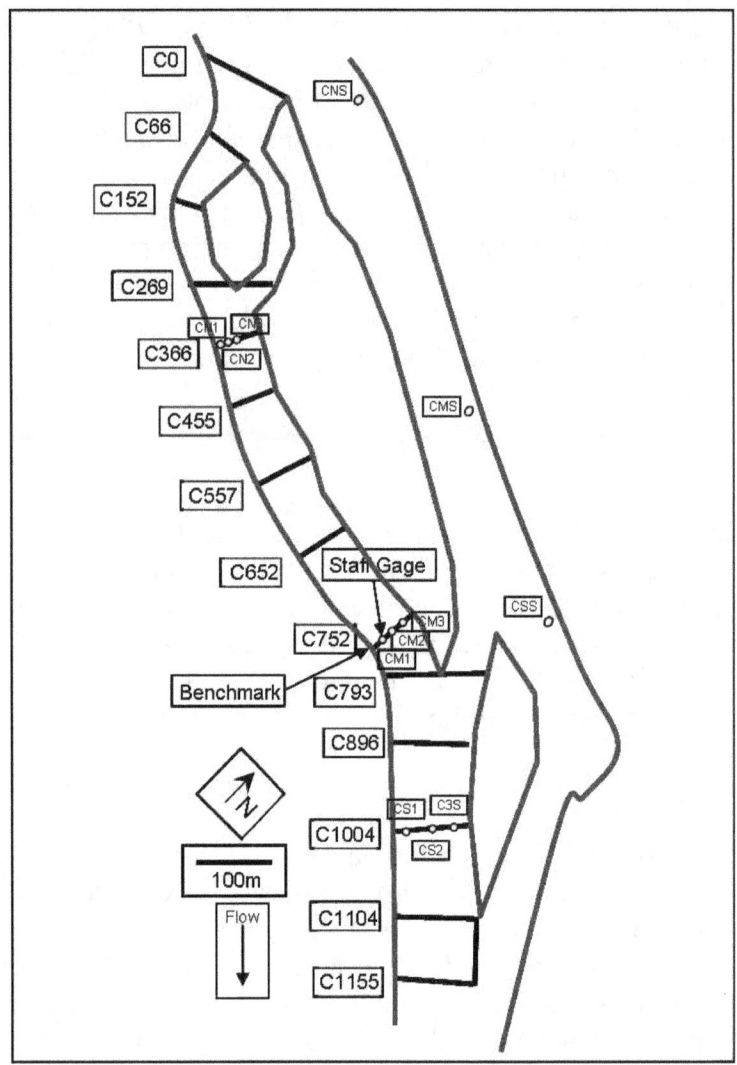

Figure 5. Site map of Site 3, showing transect layout, transect name, and staff gage and benchmark locations. Yellow dots represent temperature data logger locations and are labeled with identification name.

Bathymetry Data

Bathymetry measurements were collected at each of the three sites during the summer of 2004 and again during summer, 2005. Bathymetry at each site was measured relative to the elevations of permanent concrete site benchmarks that were installed along the bank prior to data collection. Each transect was divided into segments using a metric tape measure, and the contour of the river bottom was measured across each transect using a survey level (David White Meridian L6-20, Watseka, IL) (Figure 6). A compass was used to measure the orientation of each transect and these values were later used along with bathymetry data to create a bathymetric map of the site. Contour measurements were taken every 3 m (9.84 ft) across each transect unless a noticeable change in bottom contour was observed, in which case additional measurements were collected.

Temperature Data

Nine temperature data loggers (Optical StowAway Temp, Onset Computer Corporation, Bourne, MA) were installed at each site from July–December 2004 and March–November 2005 (Figures. 3–5). At *A. heterodon* sites, three loggers were installed and anchored to the river bottom at each of three transects in the upper, middle, and lower portions of the site. The middle row of data loggers were placed along the nearest transect to the *A. heterodon* locations. Three temperature data loggers were also installed in three separate locations in each corresponding surrogate site. The surrogate sites were chosen based upon proximity to the mussel sites as well as the degree to which the surrogate mimicked the mussel site layout. All data loggers were programmed to record temperature every 30 minutes until the available memory was filled, approximately six months. These data were later used to analyze temperature regimes at mussel and surrogate sites and to develop temperature prediction models. In order to enable comparisons of temperature data measured at the same time but on different data loggers as well as to account for differences in the measured temperature of each data logger, calibration curves were developed to correct for deviations from the "true temperature" for each data logger, as measured under controlled conditions . We define the "true temperature" as the temperature value measured during the calibration process by a digital thermometer (Traceable digital thermometer, Control Company, Friendswood, TX). The three temperatures chosen for the calibration curve were 0, 10, and 35°C (32, 50, and 95°F) which captured the range of temperature experienced in the field. The best regression model for each data logger calibration curve was applied to the field measured temperature values which allowed them to be compared to temperature values recorded by other data loggers at the same time. These calibrated temperatures were used in the analysis for this study.

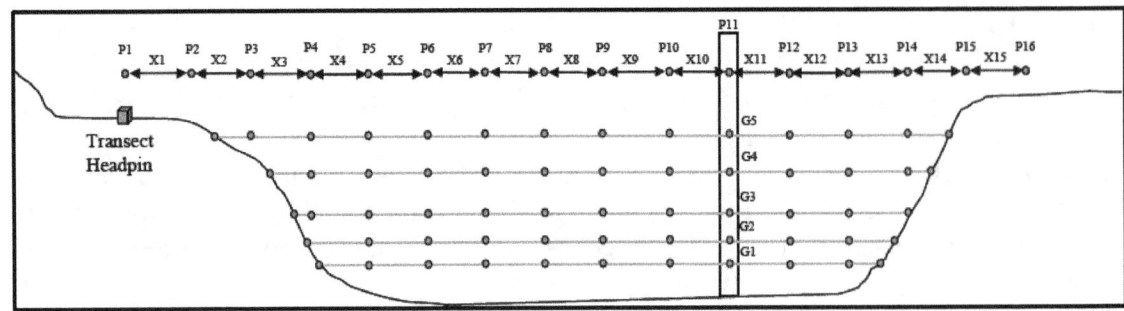

Figure 6. Cross-sectional view of typical stream transect showing method of subdividing into segment intervals. This view shows how the same transect is measured at different gage heights (G). Each data collection point is labeled P. The staff gage is shown at P11. The distance between points is labeled X and may not be uniform. The different water depths are shown on the staff gage as G.

Data Analysis

Rating Curve Development

The partial area of each transect segment and average velocity in each segment were used to calculate discharge for each segment. Total partial river discharge for the transect was then calculated for each rating event. A standard rating curve could not be applied to conditions having pooled water at zero discharge. As such, adjustments were made to the rating model based on a calculated "e" value, the gage height value corresponding to the water depth when zero discharge of water is passing through the site (Fenton and Keller 2001; Vandermeer, Hoffman, et al. 2001). For each site, this calculated "e" value was subtracted from the measured gage height (G) to account for this depth of pooled water. To develop a rating curve for each site, the stage (G-e) and corresponding total discharge (Q) for each rating event were plotted against each other in ordinate scaled graphs. Power function regression lines were fit to the data of Site 1 and Site 3 to predict discharge (Q) as a function of stage (G-e). Because Site 2 was located along the PA bank in the mainstem of the river rather than in an island channel, we created a rating curve for both the site (measured 34 m [111.5 ft] from the western bank) as well as for the mainstem river. At the fairly low discharge levels measured in this study, the relationship between stage and discharge was approximately linear for both Site 2 as well as the full river, so a linear regression line was fit to the Site 2 data. Additional gage height measurements, collected independent of the rating curve data, were then entered into the rating curve function for each site in order to generate additional discharge values that were then used in developing USGS gage-based site discharge prediction models.

12

Discharge Prediction Model Development

Models were developed to predict discharge at each site based upon USGS gages located near all three *A. heterodon* sites. For each study site, discharge values generated from the site rating curve were graphed against USGS discharge values. To avoid model overfitting and unverifiable predictions, the model was developed and applied only for gage height measurements falling plus or minus 20 percent of the measured data range. A series of linear regressions were developed using different USGS gages to evaluate the predictive ability of each. Resulting goodness-of-fit values (R^2) were compared to determine which model was most predictive of discharge for the particular mussel site. No gage was present on the mainstem Delaware River upstream of the three study sites, so we added discharge values for the Fishs Eddy gage (#01421000) located on the East Branch, and the Hale Eddy gage (#01426500) located on the West Branch, to create a combined upstream USGS gage discharge value. A second USGS gage at Callicoon (#01427510), the nearest gage downstream of all three *A. heterodon* sites, was also used.

We explored the benefits of using time lagged USGS discharge data from the upstream sites to develop site discharge prediction models, but these were not found to improve the precision of the prediction models. This study focused primarily on low flow conditions, whereas time-lagged discharge is likely to be more important for predicting discharge at higher flows. We also adjusted USGS Callicoon gage discharge values to account for likely inputs from Callicoon Creek into the Delaware River mainstem, as Callicoon Creek enters the mainstem river downstream from Hale Eddy and Fishs Eddy but upstream of the USGS Callicoon gage. A gage station located in the lower section of Callicoon Creek stopped functioning sometime between 2000 and 2002, so that only stage was recorded for Callicoon Creek during the study period. We developed a provisional rating curve from periodic rating event data collected by the USGS following the gage failure in an attempt to determine the discharge value from Callicoon Creek. There were noticeable changes in discharge values between the USGS 2004 and 2005 data, so separate rating curves were developed for each year. We applied the provisional rating equations to the existing stage data recorded at the Callicoon Creek gage, and subtracted these values from the USGS Callicoon gage on the Delaware River to account for approximate input from Callicoon Creek. Then, discharge values generated by applying each mussel site rating curve to the additional gage heights measurements were graphed against these new adjusted discharge values at the USGS Callicoon gage. The predictive ability of these adjusted USGS Callicoon gage models was compared to its corresponding unadjusted model using goodness-of-fit values (R^2) for these adjusted and unadjusted models to determine whether predictive ability improved using the adjusted data. The best site discharge prediction model was identified as the one with the highest goodness-of-fit value.

Bathymetric Mapping

A GPS unit (GPS V, Garmin International Inc., Olathe, Kansas) was used to determine the elevation above mean sea level of benchmarks at each mussel site. Contour values at each site, measured relative to each site benchmark, were then converted to values of elevation above sea level for referencing purposes. Differences between 2004 and 2005 elevation values (i.e. delta values) were calculated to determine the magnitude of any deposition and scouring across transects at each site between years as a result of flooding. The orientation of each transect, along with delta values and corresponding elevation above sea level values, were used to create three-dimensional maps of all the sites. Bathymetry data from 2005 were then used to generate water depth profiles for all three sites under three conditions: 1) the zero discharge stage condition; 2) the stage corresponding to minimal wetted perimeter (P_{min}); and 3) the stage corresponding to fully wetted perimeter (P_{full}).

Wetted Perimeter Analysis

The primary goal of the wetted perimeter (P) analysis was to determine what value of wetted perimeter would be required at each *A. heterodon* site to: 1) maintain a water depth of 10 cm (3.94 in) above the shallowest known *A. heterodon* locations within each site, thereby protecting existing mussels; or 2) maintain a water depth of 10 cm (3.94 in) at the shallowest locations known to support mussels of any species within each site, thereby protecting entire mussel habitat areas within each site. *Alasmidonta heterodon* were never found in less than 10 cm (3.94 in) of water in the Delaware River (W. Lellis, USGS, unpublished data), so this depth was used as the minimum water depth target within *A. heterodon* habitat. The first condition would provide sufficient inundation (at least 10 cm [3.94 in]) to protect *A. heterodon* at known locations, thereby protecting mussels and existing habitat. We defined this first P value as the minimal wetted perimeter value (P_{min}). The second condition would allow for submersion (at least 10 cm [3.94 in]) to protect mussels of all species and habitat known to occur within the sites and the corresponding P value was defined as the fully wetted perimeter value (P_{full}). This P_{full} could account for minor shifts in the existing population locations protecting *A. heterodon* from being dewatered during changing river conditions.

At a given stage, P was determined by measuring distance along the bottom of the river below the surface of the water using a two-dimensional map of the staff gage transect. P was measured at each 5 cm (2 in) depth increment for the range of gage height (G) values incorporated in the site rating curve plus 20%. For Site 1 this range was 0.0–1.1 m (0.0–43.3 in), for Site 2 this range was 0.0–0.8 m (0–31.5 in), and for Site 3 this range was 0.0–1.1 m (0.0–43.3 in). Site stage values (G-e) were then converted to site discharge (Q) values using the respective site rating curve. Ordinate-scale graphs with Q as the independent variable and P as the dependent variable were created to depict how the wetted perimeter value varied in response to changes in site discharge.

For each site, points representing known *A. heterodon* locations were identified and the corresponding elevation above sea level (ESL) values were identified for each point using the nearest site transect. The gage height corresponding to this ESL value was also determined. A water depth of 10 cm (3.94 in) was added to this gage height to identify the stage corresponding to the P_{min}. The second P value at each site (P_{full}) corresponded to the gage height needed to maintain 10 cm (3.94 in) of water over shallowest areas (or areas of highest elevation) known to contain mussels of any species in each site. These points were identified using mussel location data from the most recent survey data (2002 quantitative mussel survey, W. Lellis, USGS, unpublished data). We identified the single shallowest point and corresponding ESL along any transect where mussels occurred in each site. For Site 1 this point was on transect F333 (Figure 4). For Site 2, the point occurred in transect H0 (Figure 5). For Site 3, the shallowest point containing mussels occurred on transect C269 (Figure 6). Next, the gage heights corresponding to these elevations were identified at each site. We added 10 cm (3.94 in) to this gage height to determine the stage that would correspond with a water depth of 10 cm (3.94 in) at the shallowest mussel location. Site rating curves were used to calculate the corresponding site discharge to these identified stage values. These site discharge levels were used in conjunction with the discharge prediction models to determine the corresponding USGS gage discharge needed to maintain the defined site water depth condition.

As bathymetry data were measured at different stage conditions to create a wetted perimeter map for each site from this data a level water surface needed to be assumed throughout the entire site. As each of the sites was at least 800 m (2,624.7 ft) in length, we expected that water surface elevation would be higher at the upstream limits of each site than at the downstream limits. To account for the gradient in water surface elevations, the average water surface elevation was determined at three transects within the site using water depth values collected between 2004 and 2005 by the USGS to develop a decision support system for resource managers in the Delaware River basin (Bovee, Waddle et al. 2007). Unlike the current study, these water depth measurements were measured during a single stage condition which captured the relative water surface elevations throughout the entire site at a single stage. These three transects were the upstream and downstream transect at the site limits and the staff gage transect. If river bottom bathymetry data indicated a control structure; meaning a river feature that could backup water throughout the site, additional water surface elevations were estimated.

Using ArcGIS, water depth at six points across these transects was sampled from one of the USGS decision support system water depth profile maps at a comparable flow condition to the P_{min} level. Six points were employed to provide a representative sample across the transect. These water depth values were added to the river bottom elevation value from the current study at these same reference points resulting in the water surface elevation values. The average water surface elevation values across the three previously mentioned transects were calculated and the difference between upstream and downstream elevation values along with the distance between transects were used to calculate the elevation gradient in that portion of the site. These gradients, indicating the change in water surface elevation per meter within the site, were applied to the level water surface data for both the P_{min} and P_{full} site conditions, thereby accounting for the water surface gradient within the site.

Temperature Analysis

The objectives of the temperature analyses were to: 1) determine if within-site locations where *A. heterodon* were present differed from other within-site locations and surrogate sites where no *A. heterodon* were present; 2) determine if within-site temperatures can be predicted using data from established thermal gages; and 3) determine if within-site temperature deviations are related to mainstem discharge. Because high temperatures were the focus of this study, all analyses were conducted using 6 pm data, corresponding to the average time of daily high mean water temperature according to USGS gage data.

Temperature patterns within each site were analyzed with respect to the temperature at the data loggers nearest to the known *A. heterodon* locations. The objective of this analysis was to determine whether the mussel locations within the site differed from the rest of the site. For Site 1 the base logger was located at the staff gage (FM1) within the site (Figure 3). For Site 2, the data logger at the staff gage (HM1) and the logger nearest the Pennsylvania bank in the southern row (HS1) were both near the mussels and either one could have represented the *A. heterodon* location (Figure 4). Analyses of temperatures from HS1 and HM1 revealed no difference between the temperature data, so data from the logger at the staff gage (HM1) were used. For Site 3, the middle logger (CM2) along the staff gage transect was used in the analysis (Figure 5).

Data from the upper, middle, and downstream rows as well as surrogate locations of data loggers were evaluated first by regressing 6 pm temperature for the non-mussel site against that of the mussel site to determine the extent to which temperatures within a site varied consistently where mussels were present and absent. Deviations from the one-to-one line in the ordinate-scale graphs for the regression indicated temperature differences between within-site locations under similar river conditions. Following this, two-way analysis of variance (ANOVA, SAS 9.1, Proc MIXED) using time as a blocking variable was performed with the data for each thermister evaluated in relation to all the other within-site locations. The null hypothesis #1 (Ho) being tested by the two-way ANOVA was that temperatures directly above the substrate were uniform throughout each *A. heterodon* site. All two-way ANOVA tests were considered significant at the $\alpha=0.05$ level.

The ability of established gages to predict temperatures at *A. heterodon* sites was assessed using thermal stations at Kellams Bridge (#01427301) and Callicoon (#01427510). Because temperature data was not available from the USGS Callicoon gage during 2004, we only used 2005 data for this portion of the analysis. These analyses were conducted using only measurements for which all sites (the mussel site of interest, Kellams Bridge and Callicoon) had simultaneous data available. This allowed a complete comparison of data from Kellams Bridge and the USGS Callicoon gage for the same times. For each study site, temperature values from the thermal logger nearest the highest density of *A. heterodon* at that site were graphed against mainstem thermal station values. A series of linear regressions were then applied and the resulting goodness-of-fit values (R^2) used to determine which model best predicted temperature for the particular mussel site.

Finally, the relationship between mainstem discharge and site temperature deviation was evaluated by first calculating daily differences in 6 pm temperatures between *A. heterodon* sites using the Kellams Bridge thermal station for Sites 1 and 2 and the USGS Callicoon gage for Site 3. We then compared the deviation in site temperature from mainstem to the daily discharge at the USGS Callicoon gage. We expected to see a trend characterized by decreasing differences between site temperature and mainstem temperature as mainstem discharge levels increase. This would indicate the optimal discharge level necessary to minimize river effects on site thermal properties. When no significant trends were observed, we sorted temperature data into three ranges to focus on summer and winter temperature extremes: 0.00–7.99°C (32.00–46.38°F [Group A]), 8.00–20.99°C (46.4–69.78°F [Group B]), and 21.00–32.00°C (69.80–89.60°F [Group C]). Groups A and C were of particular interest, as they included extreme winter and summer temperatures, respectively. As in the ungrouped analysis, an ordinate-scale graph was created for each site with site deviation as the dependent variable and discharge at the USGS Callicoon gage as the independent variable.

Flow Analysis

Discharge Prediction Models

There were no marked improvements in the goodness-of-fit measures (R^2) when adjustments were made for inputs from Callicoon Creek to the USGS Callicoon discharge data (Table 2). As a consequence, we did not use the Callicoon Creek adjustments in our evaluations.

Site 1: The Site 1 model had nearly the same level of predictive ability regardless of whether the USGS Callicoon gage model (R^2=0.85) or the combined Fishs Eddy + Hale Eddy gages (R^2=0.88) were used (Table 3, Figure 7). The Site 1 discharge prediction model based upon the combined discharge from both USGS Fishs Eddy + Hale Eddy gages was:

$$y = 0.43 \ x - 1.60 \ (R^2 = 0.88) \ \text{(Figure 7)}$$
y= Site 1 discharge, cms,
x= USGS Fishs Eddy + Hale Eddy discharges, cms.

The Site 1 discharge prediction model based upon the USGS Callicoon gage was:

$$y = 0.49 \ x - 3.12 \ (R^2 = 0.85) \ \text{(Figure 7)}$$
y= Site 1 discharge, cms,
x= USGS Callicoon gage discharge, cms.

Site 2: The model based upon the USGS Callicoon gage discharge (R^2=0.96) better predicted discharge at Site 2 than the model based upon the USGS Fishs Eddy gage + Hale Eddy gage discharge combination (R^2=0.64) (Table 3, Figure 8). The Site 2 discharge prediction model based upon the combined discharge from both USGS Fishs Eddy + Hale Eddy gages was:

$$y = 0.13x + 0.20 \ (R^2 = 0.64) \ \text{(Figure 8)}$$
y= Site 2 discharge, cms,
x= Fishs Eddy + Hale Eddy discharges, cms.

The Site 2 discharge prediction model based upon the USGS Callicoon gage was:

$$y = 0.11x + 0.33 \ (R^2 = 0.96) \ \text{(Figure 8)}$$
y= Site 2 discharge, cms,
x= USGS Callicoon discharge, cms.

Table 2. Goodness-of-fit estimates (R^2) for discharge prediction models created utilizing USGS Callicoon gage data compared to gage data corrected for Callicoon Creek water inputs.

Site	USGS Callicoon gage	
	Uncorrected	Corrected
Site 1	0.88	0.87
Site 2	0.86	0.87
Site 3	0.93	0.88

Table 3. Summary table of USGS discharge values (cms, R^2 value) corresponding to the occlusion of point of *Alasmidonta heterodon* sites. The discharge prediction models were developed using only 2005 data.

Site	Zero Discharge Stage Height Condition	
	USGS Fishs Eddy + Hale Eddy gage	USGS Callicoon gage
Site 1	3.7 (R^2=0.88)	6.4 (R^2=0.85
Site 2	0.0 (R^2=0.64)	0.0 (R^2=0.96)
Site 3	15.1 (R^2=0.86)	12.8 (R^2=0.96)

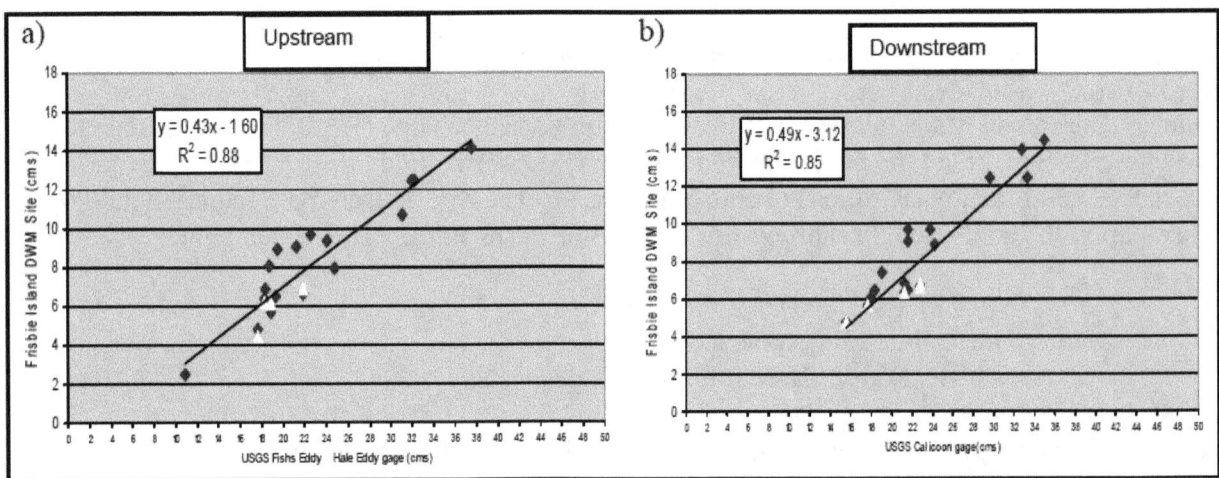

Figure 7. Relationship between Site 1 discharge and USGS gage stations: a) Fishs Eddy and Hale Eddy combined gage discharge; and b) USGS Callicoon gage discharge. Yellow triangle data points are measured rating curve data and the blue diamond data points are discharge values calculated using the developed site rating curve.

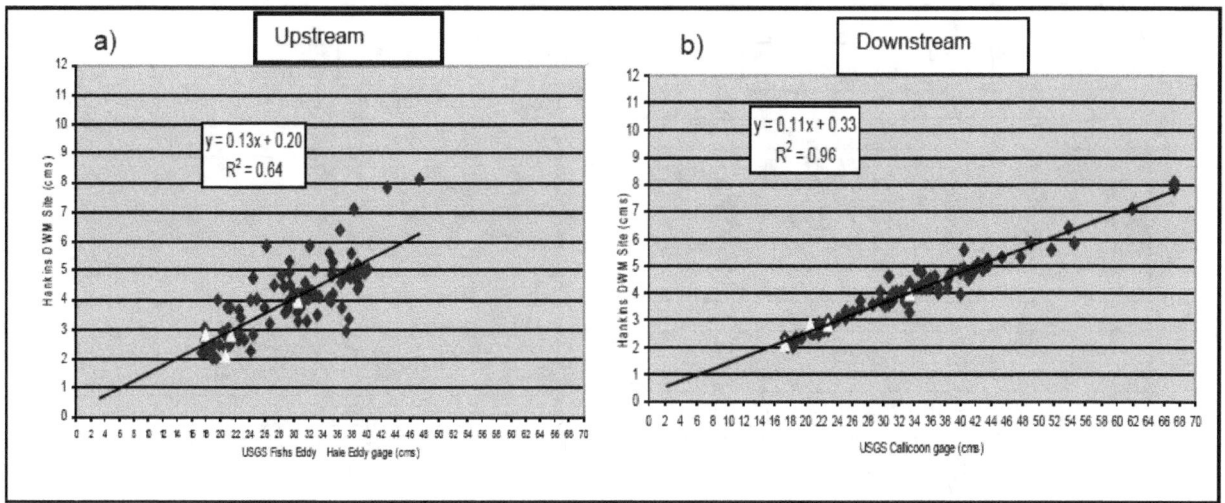

Figure 8. Relationship between Site 2 discharge and USGS gage stations: a) Fishs Eddy and Hale Eddy combined gage discharge; and b) USGS Callicoon gage discharge. Yellow triangle data points are measured rating curve data and the blue diamond data points are discharge values calculated using the developed site rating curve and visually measured gage height values.

Site 3: The USGS Callicoon gage (R^2=0.96) better predicted Site 3 discharge than the USGS Fishs Eddy + Hale Eddy; (R^2=0.87) (Table 3, Figure 9). The Site 3 discharge prediction model based upon the combined discharge from both USGS Fishs Eddy + Hale Eddy gages was:

$y = 0.54x - 8.37$ (R^2=0.86) (Figure 9)
$\quad$ y= Site 3 discharge, cms,
$\quad$ x= Fishs Eddy + Hale Eddy discharges, cms.

The Site 3 discharge prediction model based upon the USGS Callicoon gage was:

$y = 0.33x - 4.27$ (R^2=0.96) (Figure 9)
$\quad$ y= Site 3 discharge, cms,
$\quad$ x= USGS Callicoon discharge, cms.

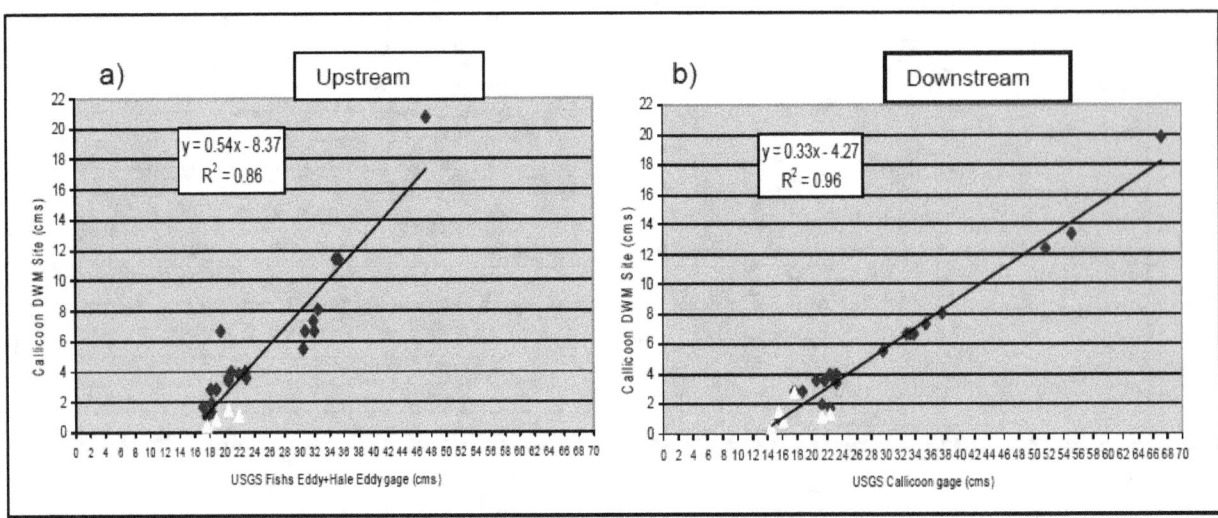

Figure 9. Relationship between Site 3 discharge and USGS gage stations: a) Fishs Eddy and Hale Eddy combined gage discharge; and b) USGS Callicoon gage discharge. Yellow triangle data points are measured rating curve data and the blue diamond data points are discharge values calculated using the developed site rating curve.

Bathymetry Analysis

Site 1:

At zero discharge at Site 1 (corresponding to 6.4 cms [226.01 cfs] discharge at the USGS Callicoon gage), the upstream end of the site has limited standing water (0.0–0.25 m [0.00–9.84 in]) (Figure 10). Under these conditions, all of the *A. heterodon* mussel locations identified in 2002 appear to be somewhat protected from dewatering and desiccation, as they occur within areas of fairly shallow water (0.01–1.0 m [0.39–39.37 in]). Such areas extend throughout most of the site. Despite minor changes in bathymetry between the 2004 and 2005 surveys at Site 1 (Figure 11) no noticeable changes were observed in either the rating curve relationship or the site zero discharge stage between years.

The relationship between wetted perimeter (P) and discharge (Q) was evaluated for Site 1 using a range of adjusted site stage values (G-e) which correspond to site discharge values (Q) between 0.0–22.2 cms (0.0–783.99 cfs [Table 4, Figure 12]). This range of Q values yielded corresponding P values of 48.0–71.3 m (157.48–233.92 ft). The minimal wetted perimeter (P_{min}) value needed to maintain the identified target of 10 cm water at known *A. heterodon* locations within Site 1 corresponded to a stage value of 0.30 m. This was equivalent to a site Q of 0.80 cms (28.3 cfs) and a P_{min} of 60.3 m (197.83 ft), and also maintained water to the base of the bank (Figure 13). This Q value constituted only 3% of the maximum site discharge (Q_t) analyzed while the P_{min} constituted 85% of the maximum site wetted perimeter (P_t), suggesting that significant potential mussel habitat across this transect is available under most site discharge levels and is most likely a pool. The calculated USGS Callicoon gage discharge rate needed to maintain the site P_{min} is 9.7 cms (342.5 cfs).

20

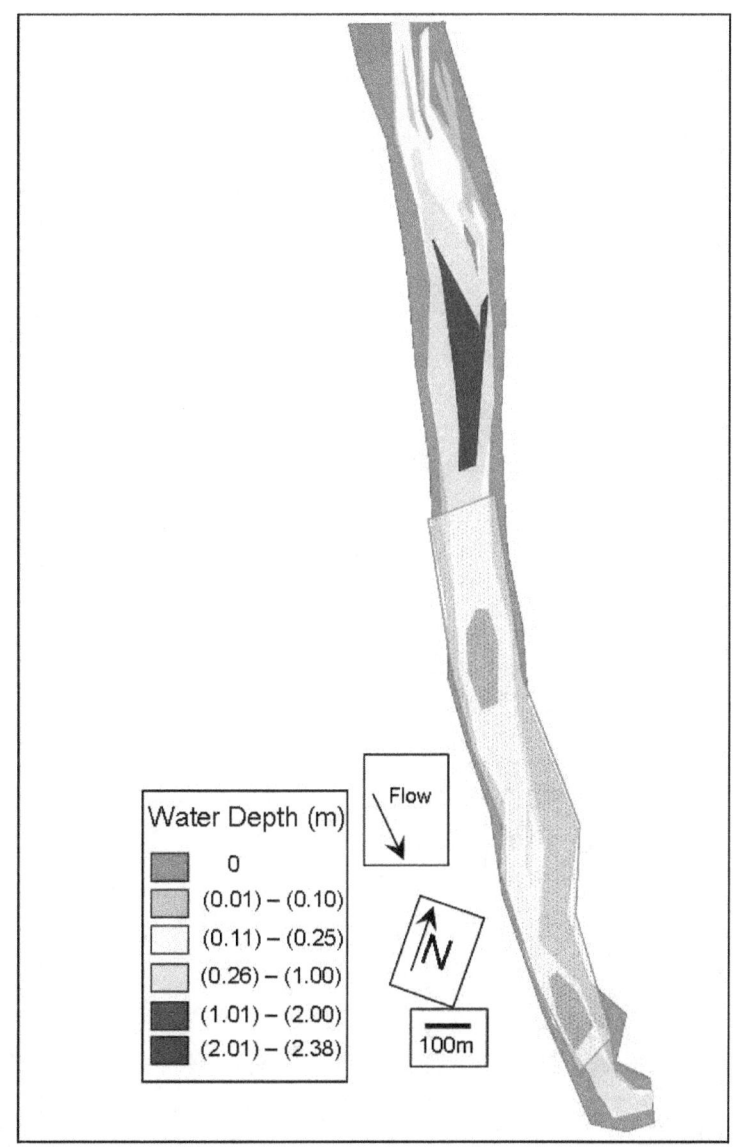

Figure 10. Map of Site 1 showing water depth (m) conditions when the site is at zero discharge stage conditions (discharge at USGS Callicoon = 6.4 cms). Grey dotted area represents area known to contain *Alasmidonta heterodon* during summer 2002.

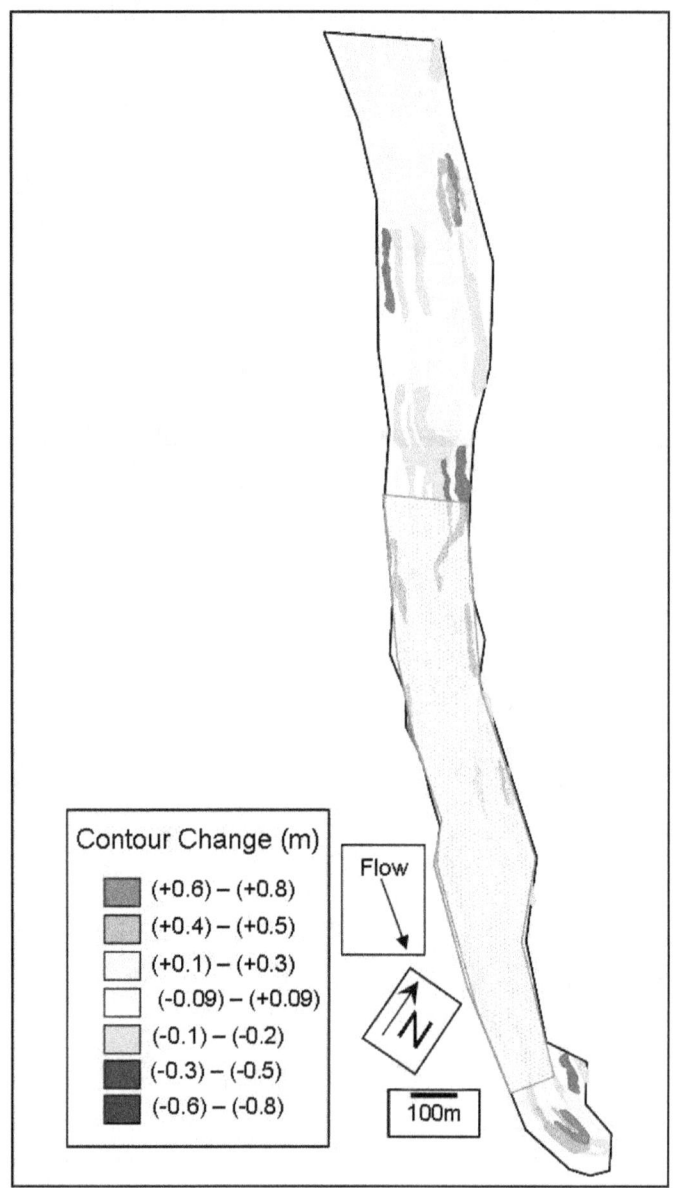

Figure 11. Map of Site 1 showing changes in bathymetry measurements (m) between the 2004 and 2005 surveys. Grey dotted area represents area known to contain *Alasmidonta heterodon* during summer 2002.

Table 4. Site 1: stage (G-e), site discharge (Q), percentage of total site discharge (Qₜ), wetted perimeter (P), and percentage of total wetted perimeter analyzed (Pₜ) which were included in the developed P-Q site relationship. The range of G analyzed for the wetted perimeter analysis included the range of values in the site rating curve +20%. The G corresponding to the site minimal wetted perimeter (P_{min}), fully wetted perimeter (P_{full}), and associated Q value are indicated in bold.

G-e	Q	Qₜ	P	Pₜ	
(m)	(cms)	(%)	(m)	(%)	
0.00	0.0	0	48.0	67	
0.10	0.0	0	51.5	72	
0.20	0.3	1	55.5	78	
0.30	**0.8**	**3**	**60.3**	**85**	(P_{min})
0.40	1.6	7	63.8	89	
0.50	2.9	13	66.0	93	
0.55	**3.7**	**17**	**66.5**	**93**	(P_{full})
0.60	4.6	21	67.3	94	
0.70	6.9	31	68.5	96	
0.80	9.7	44	69.0	97	
0.90	13.2	59	70.0	98	
1.00	17.3	78	70.5	99	
1.10	22.2	100	71.3	100	

The fully wetted perimeter (P_{full}) for Site 1, which maintains 0.25 m (9.84 in) water depth at all available habitat within the site, set to maintain water levels of at least 10 cm (3.94 in) over the shallowest mussel location within the site, was 66.5 m (218.18 ft) and corresponded to a stage value of 0.55 m (21.65 in, Table 4, Figure 14), and a site Q of 3.7 cms (130.6 cfs). This Q value constituted 44% of the maximum site discharge (Qₜ) analyzed while the P_{full} constituted 93% of the maximum site wetted perimeter (Pₜ) analyzed. The calculated USGS Callicoon gage discharge rate needed to maintain the site P_{full} is 13.9 cms (490.9 cfs).

Site 2:

At zero discharge at Site 2 (corresponding to 0.0 cms at the USGS Callicoon gage), the mainstem river has a center channel with standing water, while the upstream end of the site (defined as extending 34 m (111.55 ft) from the Pennsylvania bank, as this site is not separated from the mainstem by an island), has shallow water in many places (0.01–1.0 m [0.39–39.37 in]) (Figure 15). From the middle of the site to the downstream end there is noticeable (0.11–1.0 m [4.33–39.37 in]) standing water (indicated by yellow to dark blue colors, Figure 15). This downstream area of standing water corresponds to the locations where *A. heterodon* were found along the Pennsylvania bank. This suggests that the mussel locations within the site are in an area largely protected from dewatering.

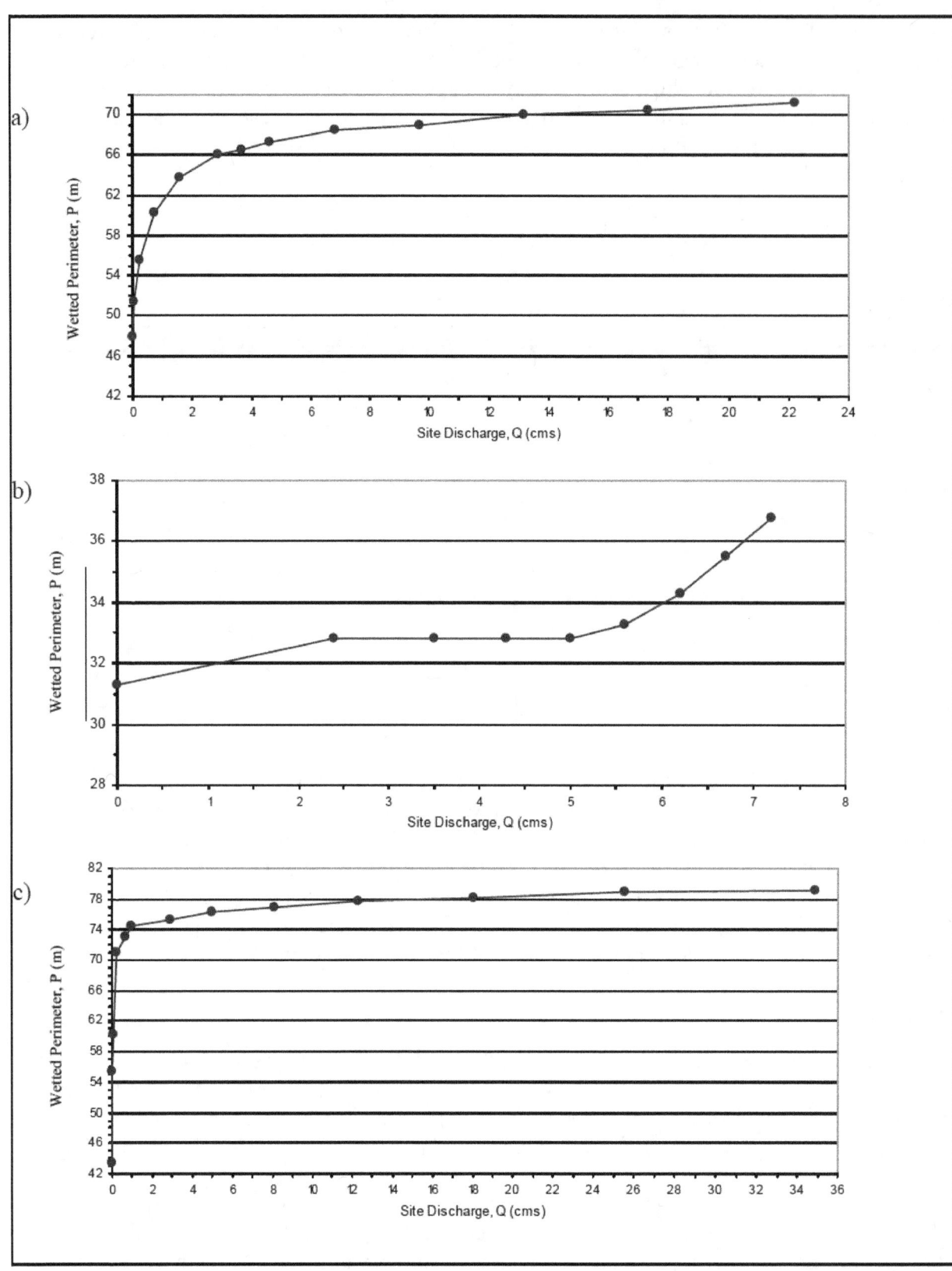

Figure 12. Ordinate-scale graph showing the wetted perimeter (P) compared to site discharge (Q) relationship for: a) Site 1; b) Site 2; and c) Site 3.

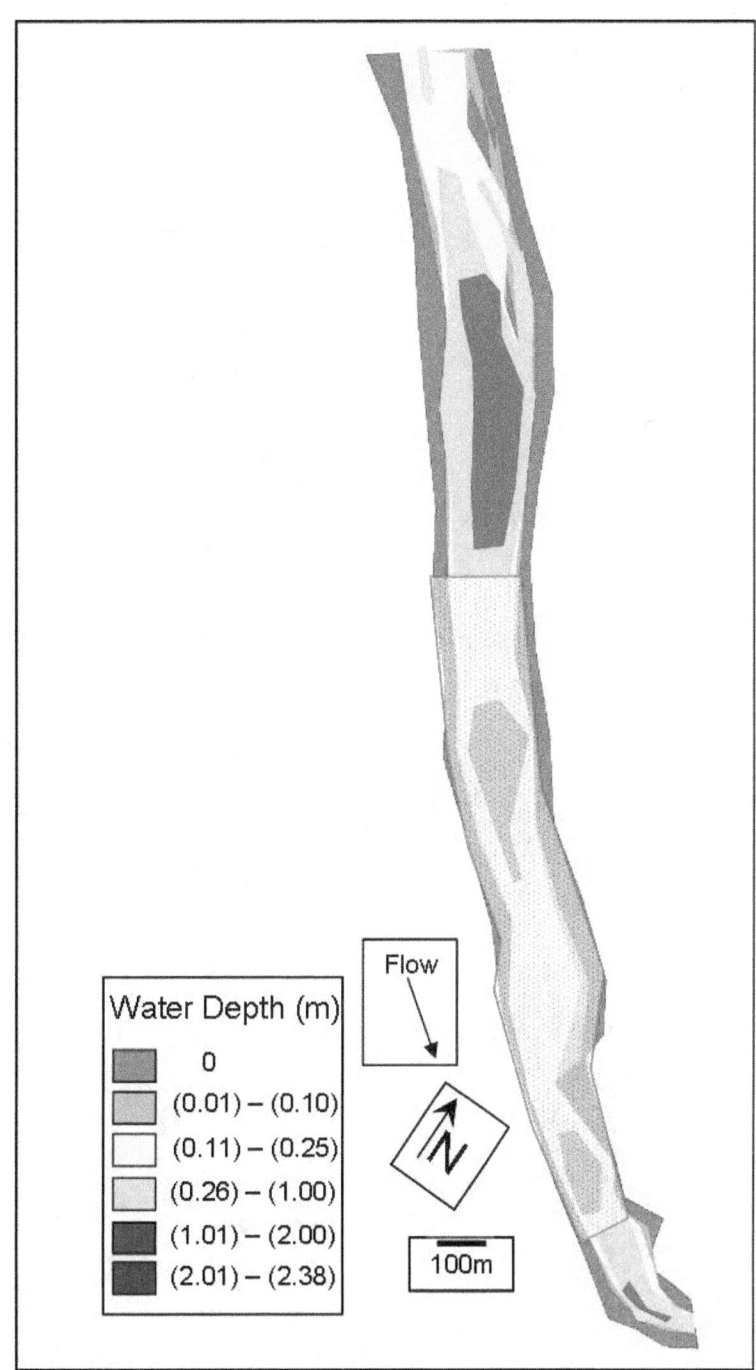

Figure 13. Map of Site 1 showing water depth (m) conditions when the minimal wetted perimeter (P_{min}) is maintained within the site (P_{min}=63.8 m, discharge at USGS Callicoon = 9.7 cms). Grey dotted area represents area known to contain *Alasmidonta heterodon* during summer 2002.

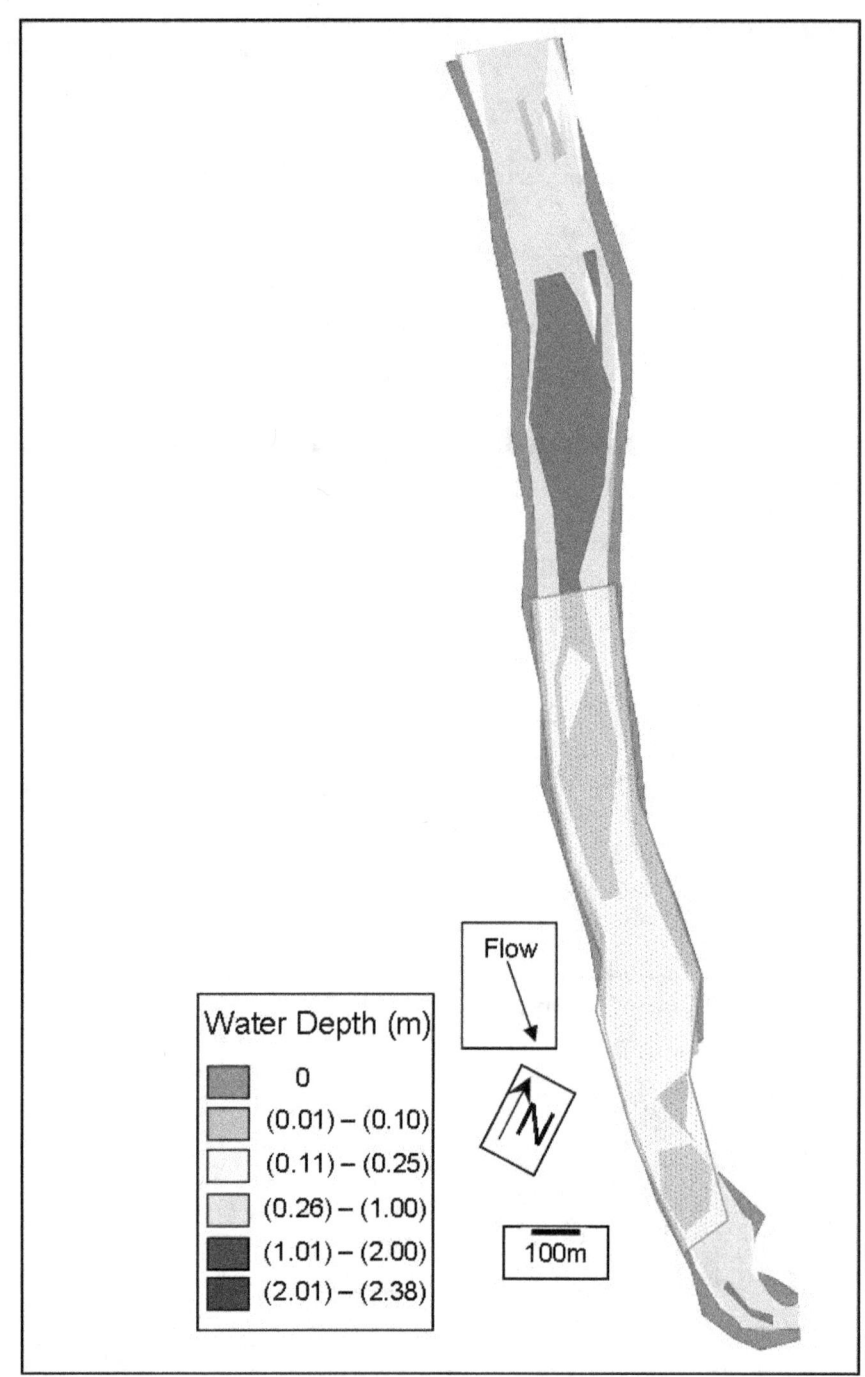

Figure 14. Map of Site 1 showing water depth (m) conditions when the fully wetted perimeter (P_{full}) is maintained within the site (P_{full}=69.0 m, discharge at USGS Callicoon = 13.9 cms). Grey dotted area represents area known to contain *Alasmidonta heterodon* during summer 2002.

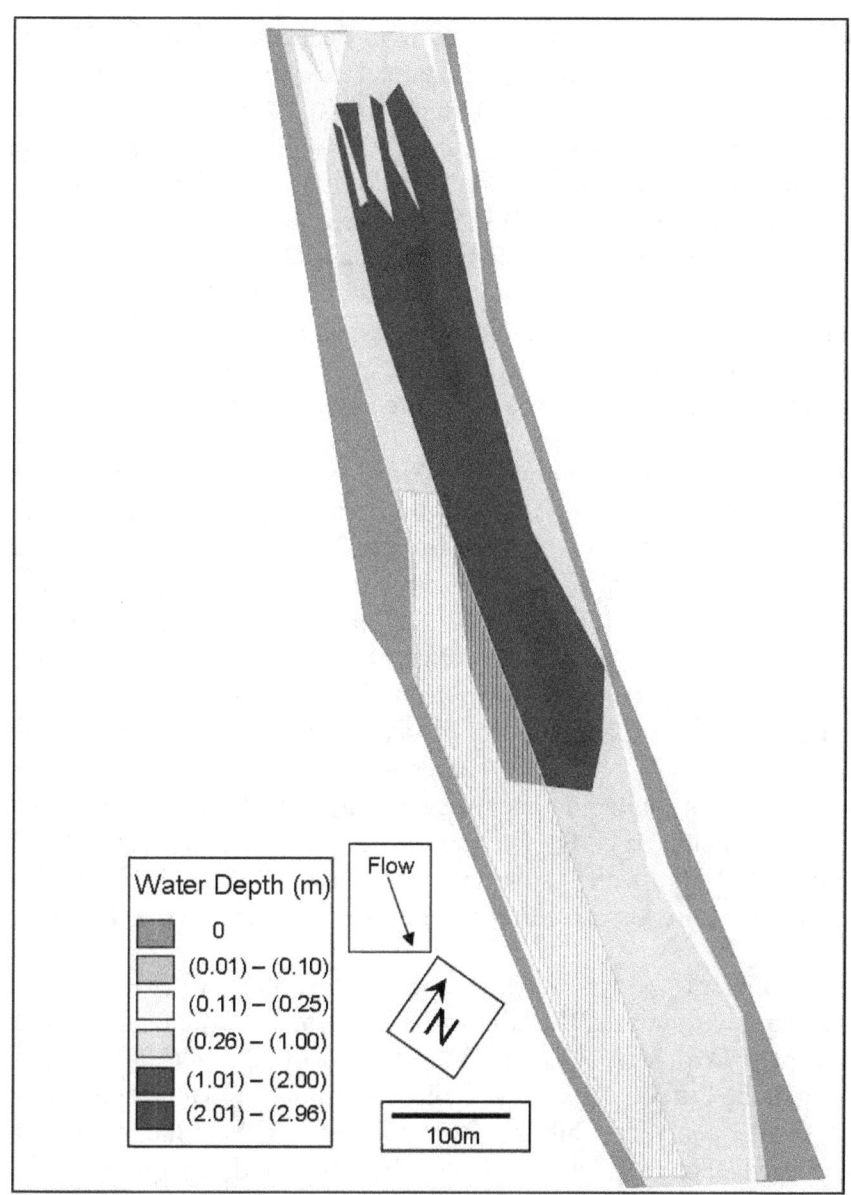

Figure 15. Map of Site 2 showing water depth (m) conditions when the site is at the zero discharge stage conditions (discharge at USGS Callicoon = 0.0 cms). Grey striped area represents area known to contain *Alasmidonta heterodon* during summer 2002.

Two major changes in river bathymetry occurred in or near Site 2 between 2004 and 2005. A large area of deposition appeared in the center channel near the upstream limit of the site, while the largest area of scouring appeared throughout most of the downstream end of the site (Figure 16). This area was characterized by slight scouring (0.1–0.2 m [3.94–7.87 in]) of material throughout the central channel with some long strips of more moderate (0.3–0.5 m [11.81–19.68 in]) to severe (0.6–0.8 m [23.62–31.50 in]) scouring towards the banks. Strips of scouring also occurred along both the New York and Pennsylvania banks in the upper reaches of the site. Bathymetry changes in the Site 2 area along the Pennsylvania bank were characterized by long strips of scouring separated by areas of no change. A majority of the locations of *A. heterodon* align with these areas where no or very little change in bathymetry occurred, indicating the mussels may be inhabiting areas where the substrate is most stable.

The relationship between P and Q determined at Site 2 was different from the relationships in Site 1 and Site 3 (Table 5, Figure 12). This may be because Site 2 is directly connected to the mainstem compared to Sites 1 and 3 which are isolated from the river by island chains. Site 2 had the smallest range of site Q values (0.0–7.2 cms [0.0–254.27 cfs]) analyzed of the three sites. The minimal wetted perimeter (P_{min}) for Site 2 (32.8 m [107.6 ft]) corresponded to a stage (G-e) of 0.310 m (1.017 ft). Therefore, a site Q of 0.78 cms (27.5 cfs) maintained 10 cm (3.94 in) of water over the known *A. heterodon* locations. From the analysis of the P to Q relationship, this Q value constituted 34% of the maximum site discharge analyzed while the P_{min} constituted 89% of the maximum site wetted perimeter (P_t), suggesting that significant potential mussel habitat along this transect is always available under site discharge levels and this area is most likely a pool (Figure 17). The calculated USGS Callicoon gage discharge rate needed to maintain the site P_{min} is 3.4 cms (120.1 cfs), which is the lowest of the three sites (Table 6). This indicates the *A. heterodon* within Site 2 are less vulnerable to dewatering than the mussels in Site 1.

The fully wetted perimeter (P_{full}) for Site 2 necessary to maintain water levels of at least 10 cm (3.94 in) over the shallowest mussel location within the site corresponded to a stage value (G-e) of 0.24 m (9.84 in), site Q of 1.9 cms (67.1 cfs) and a P_{full} of 32.5 m (106.63 ft [Table 6, Figure 18]). The analysis of the P to Q relationship indicated that this Q value constituted 28% of the maximum site discharge analyzed while the P_{full} constituted 88% of the maximum site wetted perimeter (P_t) analyzed. The calculated USGS Callicoon gage discharge rate needed to maintain the site P_{full} is 14.0 cms (494.4 cfs [Table 6]). Thus, the discharge target for P_{full} for Site 2 indicates that the shallowest mussel location in this site is likely the least vulnerable of comparable habitat in the three sites.

Site 3:

Little or no standing water (0–0.25 m [0.0–9.84 in]) is present at the upstream end of Site 3 when conditions drop to the zero discharge stage (Figure 19). Potential for dewatering at this site appears to be greater than at Sites 1 and 2. Under these conditions (corresponding to 12.8 cms [452.0 cfs] at the USGS Callicoon gage), a channel of pooled water occurs throughout the middle portion of the site. According to 2002 mussel distribution data at this site (Lellis, USGS, unpublished data), *A. heterodon* appear to occur within this area of pooled water. Flow from the other island channel also enters the site within this area. Mussels occur within this area and are likely protected from dewatering and desiccation during low flow conditions.

28

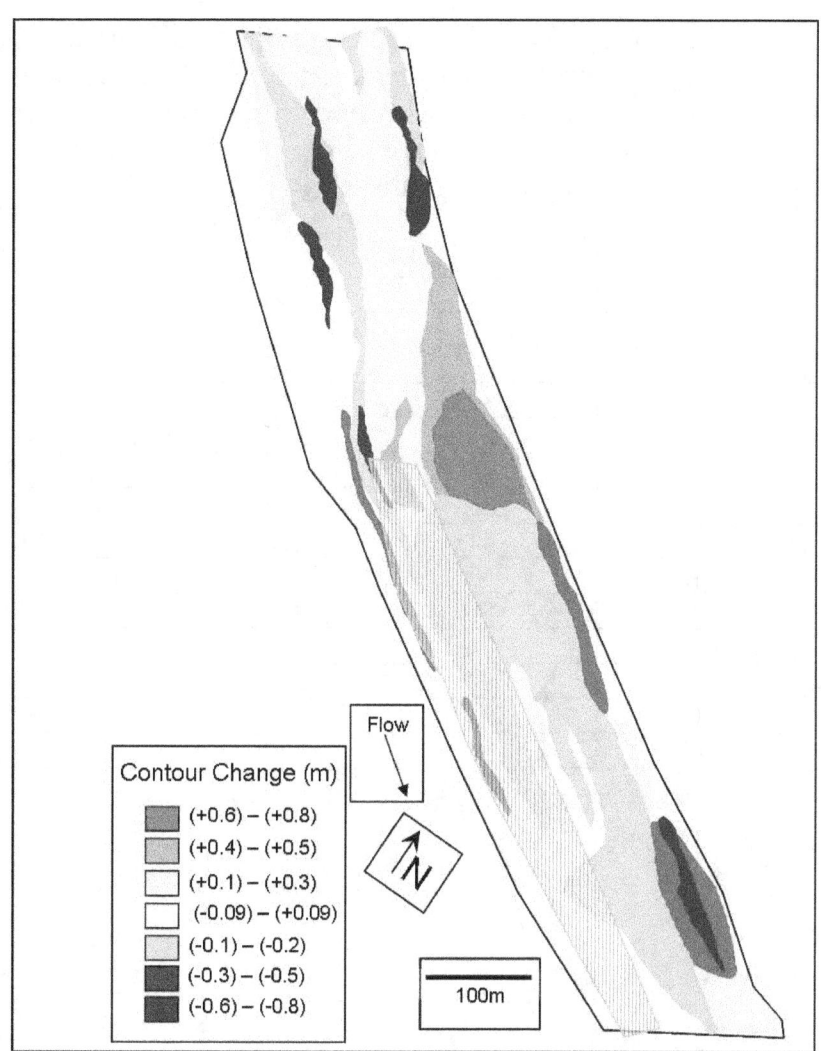

Figure 16. Map of Site 2 showing changes in bathymetry measurements (m) between the 2004 and 2005 surveys. Grey striped area represents area known to contain *Alasmidonta heterodon* during summer 2002.

Table 5. Site 2: stage (G-e), site discharge (Q), percentage of total site discharge (Q_t), wetted perimeter (P), and percentage of total wetted perimeter analyzed (P_t) which were included in the developed P-Q site relationship. The range of G analyzed for the wetted perimeter analysis included the range of values in the site rating curve +20%. The G corresponding to the site minimal wetted perimeter (P_{min}), fully wetted perimeter (P_{full}), and associated Q value are indicated in bold.

G-e	Q	Q_t	P	P_t	
(m)	(cms)	(%)	(m)	(%)	
0.00	0.00	0	30.0	82	
0.10	**0.78**	**12**	**31.3**	**85**	(P_{min})
0.20	1.56	24	32.3	88	
0.24	**1.87**	**28**	**32.5**	**88**	(P_{full})
0.30	2.34	35	32.5	88	
0.35	2.73	41	32.8	89	
0.40	3.12	47	32.8	89	
0.50	3.90	59	32.8	89	
0.60	4.68	71	3.33	90	
0.70	5.46	82	34.3	93	
0.80	6.24	94	35.5	97	
0.85	6.6	100	36.8	100	

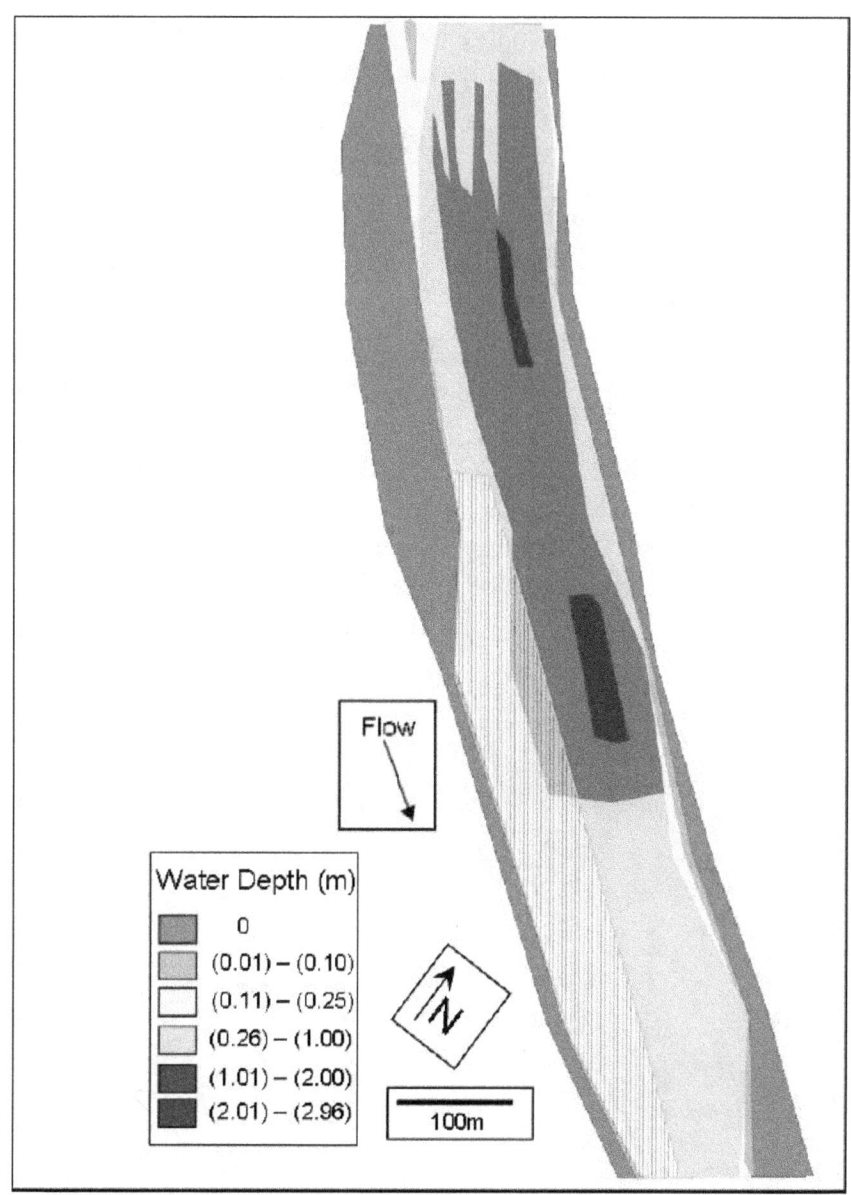

Figure 17. Map of Site 2 showing water depth (m) conditions when the minimal wetted perimeter (P_{min}) is maintained within the site (P_{min} = 31.3 m, discharge at USGS Callicoon = 3.4 cms). Grey striped area represents area known to contain *Alasmidonta heterodon* during summer 2002.

Table 6. The calculated USGS gage discharge levels (cms, R^2 value) corresponding to the minimum wetted perimeter (P_{min}) and the fully wetted perimeter (P_{full}) in each study site.

Site	Minimal Wetted Perimeter Level - P_{min}	
	USGS Fishs Eddy + Hale Eddy gage	USGS Callicoon gage
Site 1	7.5 (R^2=0.88)	9.7 (R^2=0.85)
Site 2	4.0 (R^2=0.64)	3.4 (R^2=0.96)
Site 3	17.3 (R^2=0.86)	15.8 (R^2=0.96)

Site	Fully Wetted Perimeter Level - P_{full}	
	USGS FishsEddy + Hale Eddy gage	USGS Callicoon gage
Site 1	26.4 (R^2=0.88)	13.9 (R^2=0.85)
Site 2	13.3 (R^2=0.64	14.0 (R^2=0.96)
Site 3	30.3 (R^2=0.86)	26.3 (R^2=0.96)

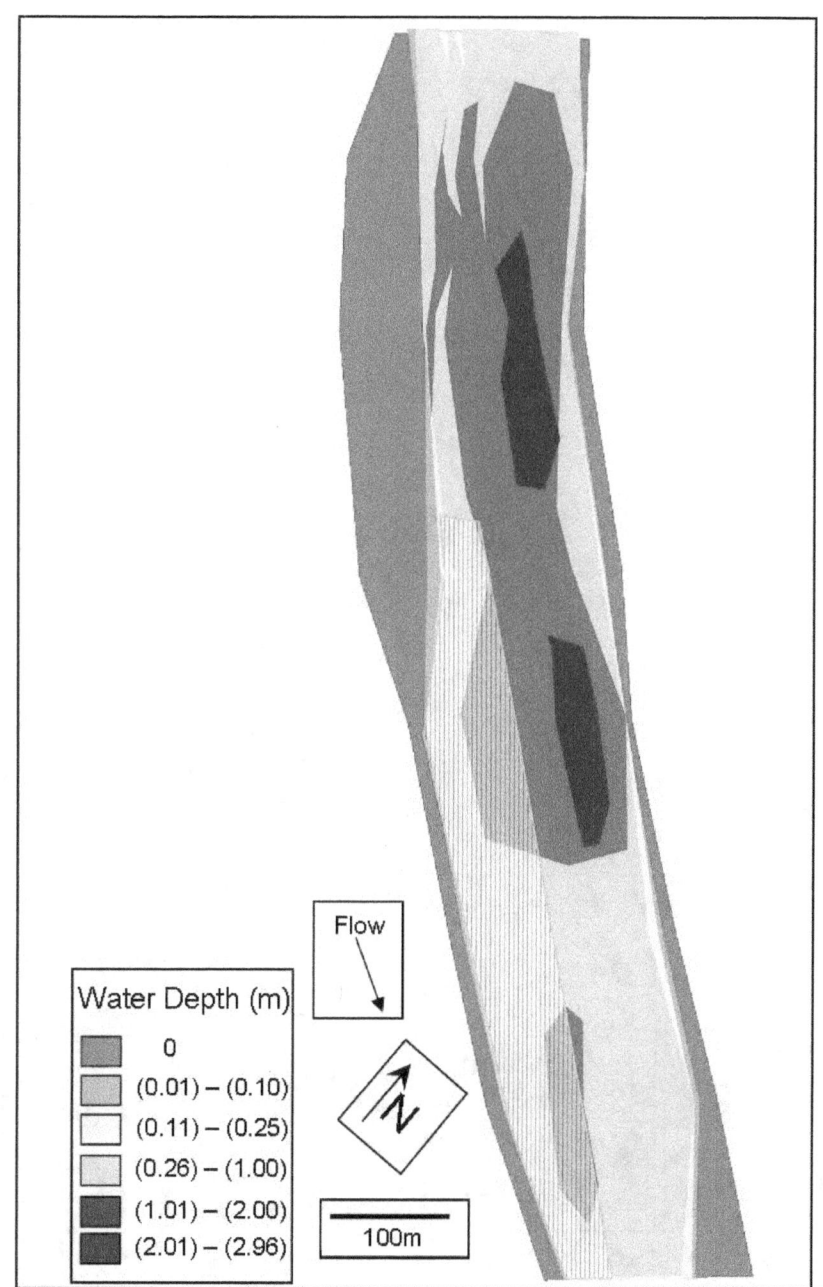

Figure 18. Map of Site 2 showing water depth (m) conditions when the fully wetted perimeter (P$_{full}$) is maintained within the site (P$_{full}$ = 32.8 m, discharge at USGS Callicoon = 14.0 cms). Grey striped area represents area known to contain *Alasmidonta heterodon* during summer 2002.

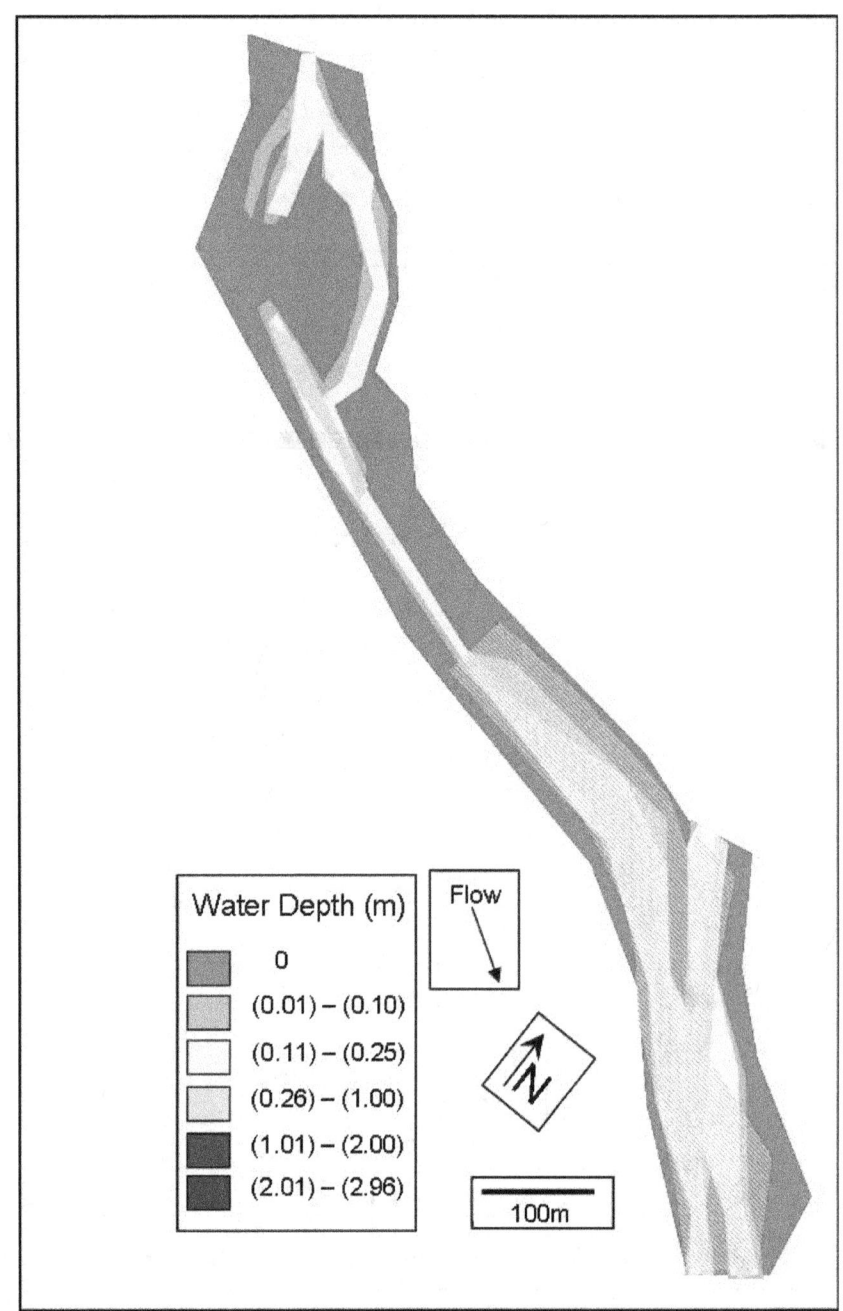

Figure 19. Map of Site 3 showing water depth (m) conditions when the site is at the zero discharge stage conditions (discharge at USGS Callicoon = 12.8 cms). Grey striped area represents area known to contain *Alasmidonta heterodon* during summer 2002.

Bathymetric changes that occurred at Site 3 between survey 2004 and 2005 were extensive. Significant deposition occurred in the upper reaches of the site, suggesting that inflow of mainstem water into the site may now be severely restricted. These bathymetric changes were measured at the upstream end of Site 3 (Figure 20), with deposition areas characterized by both moderate (0.4–0.5 m [15.75–19.68 in]) and severe (0.6–0.8 m [23.62–31.5 in]) aggradation. The remainder of the site was characterized primarily by minor scouring (0.1–0.2 m [3.94–7.87 in]) or deposition (0.1–0.3 m [3.94–11.81 in]), with small strips of slightly heavier scouring (0.3–0.5 m [11.81–19.68 in]) along most banks of the largest island in the island chain.

The P to Q relationship for Site 3 resembles that of Site 1 (Table 7, Figure 12). The ranges of Q and P were 0.0–34.9 cms (0.0–1,232.48 cfs) and 43.5–79.1 m (142.7–259.5 ft), respectively. A stage (G-e) value of 0.38 m (14.96 in) is needed to maintain the minimal wetted perimeter (P_{min}) (72.5 m [237.9 ft]) at this site. This stage value (0.38 m [14.96 in]) corresponds to a site Q value of 0.55 cms (19.4 cfs). A large percentage (92%) of the maximum P analyzed is maintained even at low discharge levels (0.55 cms [19.4 cfs]) (Figure 21). To maintain the P_{min} value (72.5 m [237.86 ft]) of Site 3 the USGS Callicoon gage discharge rate must be 15.8 cms (558.0 cfs [Table 7]).

The fully wetted perimeter (P_{full}) for Site 3 necessary to maintain water levels of at least 10 cm (3.94 in) over the shallowest mussel location within the site corresponded to a stage (G-e) of 0.58 m (22.83 in [Table 7, Figure 22]). The corresponding site Q was 2.53 cms (89.3 cfs) and a P_{full} of 76.2 m (250 ft). This Q value constituted 7% of the maximum site discharge analyzed while the P_{full} constituted 96% of the maximum site wetted perimeter (P_t) analyzed. The calculated USGS Callicoon gage discharge rate needed to maintain the site P_{full} is 26.3 cms (928.8 cfs [Table 6]).

Temperature Analysis

Temperature data loggers were installed at all nine within-site locations and three surrogate locations for summer 2004 (Figure 3, 4, and 5). At Site 1, data logger FM3 was not recovered at the end of the first data collection period. In Site 2, data logger HMS was not recovered. All data loggers were recovered at Site 3. Temperature data loggers were installed at all locations at the beginning of summer 2005. In Site 1, data loggers FN3, FM2, and FM3 were not recovered at the end of the data collection period. In Site 2, HN2, HN3, HNS, and HM3 were not recovered at the end of the period. In Site 3, only CNS was not recovered at the end of the data collection period. All temperature analyses were performed with data from the remaining temperature loggers.

Within-site Temperature Analysis

Site 1: At Site 1, water temperatures at the FS3 logger were the only observations that differed noticeably from temperatures recorded at specific within-site mussel locations (Figure 23). All other loggers recorded temperatures comparable to those at the mussel location. In particular, water temperatures at the FS3 logger location were significantly warmer, which may have been due to the presence of extremely shallow water (<0.15 m [5.9 in]) possibly subjected to warming by the sun.

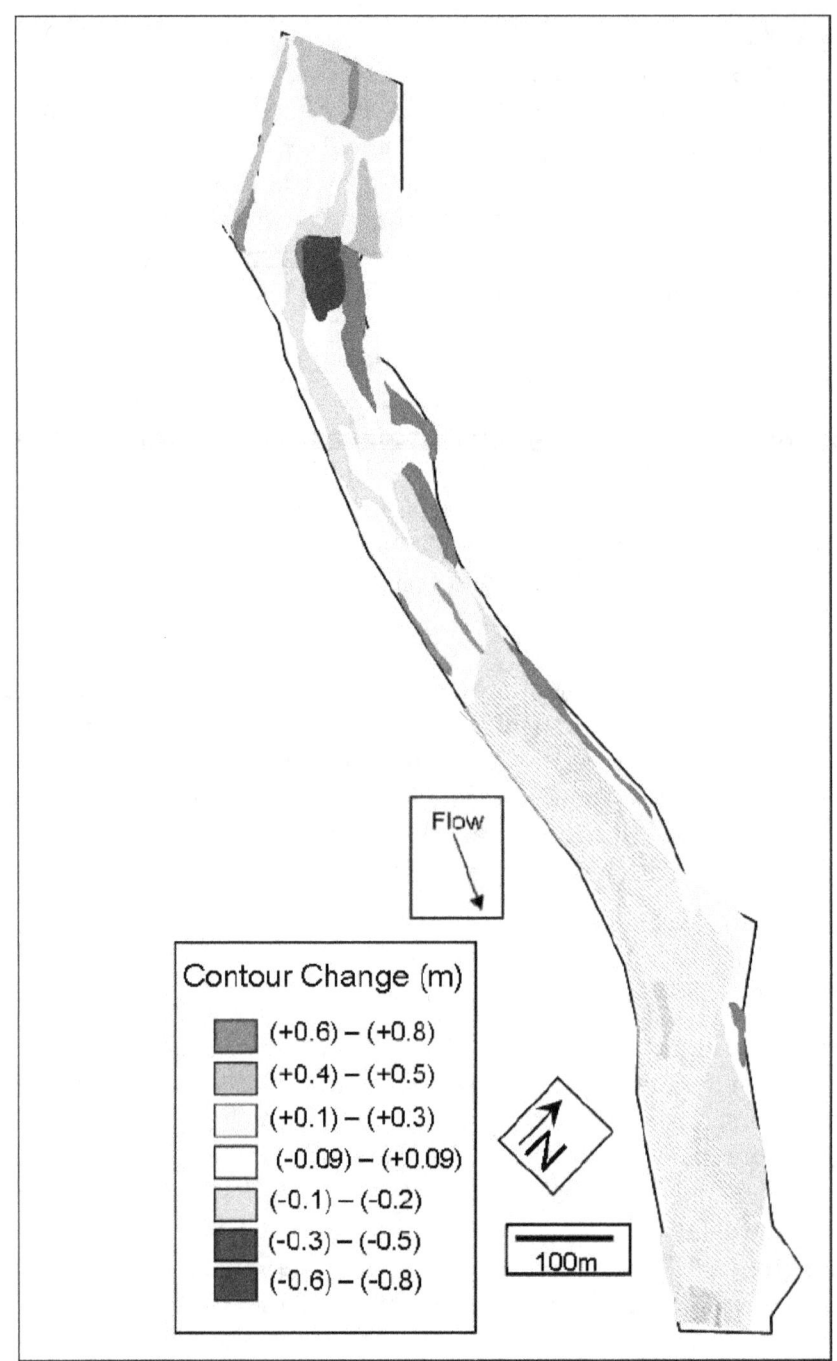

Figure 20. Map of Site 3 showing changes in bathymetry measurements (m) between the 2004 and 2005 surveys. Grey striped area represents area known to contain *Alasmidonta heterodon* during summer 2002.

Table 7. Site 3: stage (G-e), site discharge (Q), percentage of total site discharge (Q_t), wetted perimeter (P), and percentage of total wetted perimeter analyzed (P_t) which were included in the developed P-Q site relationship. The range of G analyzed for the wetted perimeter analysis included the range of values in the site rating curve +20%. The G corresponding to the site minimal wetted perimeter (P_{min}), fully wetted perimeter (P_{full}), and associated Q value are indicated in bold.

G-e	Q	Q_t	P	P_t	
(m)	(cms)	(%)	(m)	(%)	
0.00	0.00	0	43.5	55	
0.10	0.00	0	55.4	70	
0.20	0.05	0	60.3	76	
0.30	0.23	1	71.0	90	
0.38	**0.55**	**2**	**72.5**	**92**	(P_{min})
0.50	1.48	4	75.3	95	
0.58	**2.53**	**7**	**76.2**	**96**	(P_{full})
0.60	4.98	14	76.3	96	
0.70	8.06	23	77.0	97	
0.80	12.34	35	77.7	98	
0.90	18.05	52	78.1	99	
1.00	25.46	73	78.9	100	
1.10	34.85	100	79.1	100	

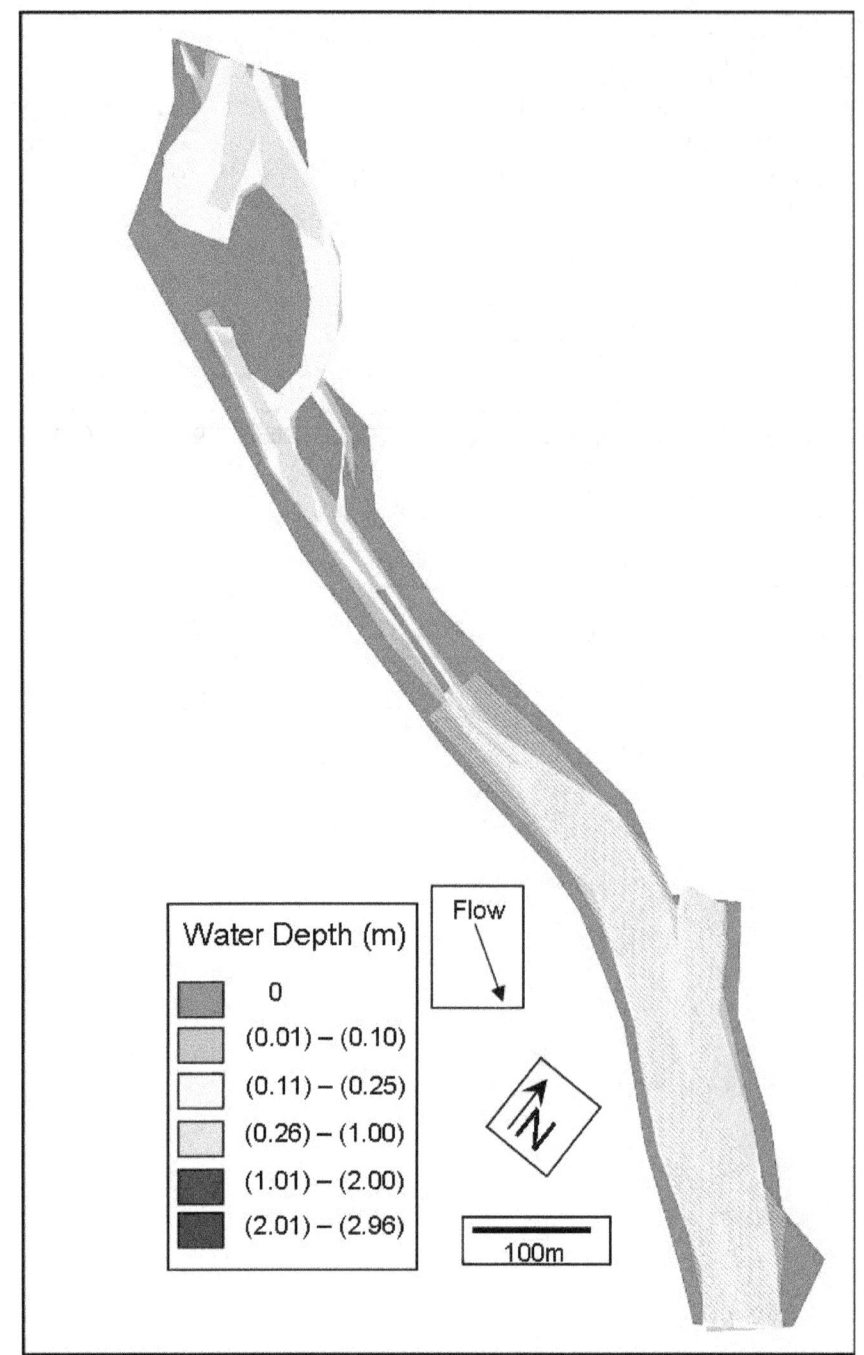

Figure 21. Map of Site 3 showing water depth (m) conditions when the minimal wetted perimeter (P_{min}) is maintained within the site (P_{min} = 74.5 m, discharge at USGS Callicoon = 15.8 cms). Grey striped area represents area known to contain *Alasmidonta heterodon* during summer 2002.

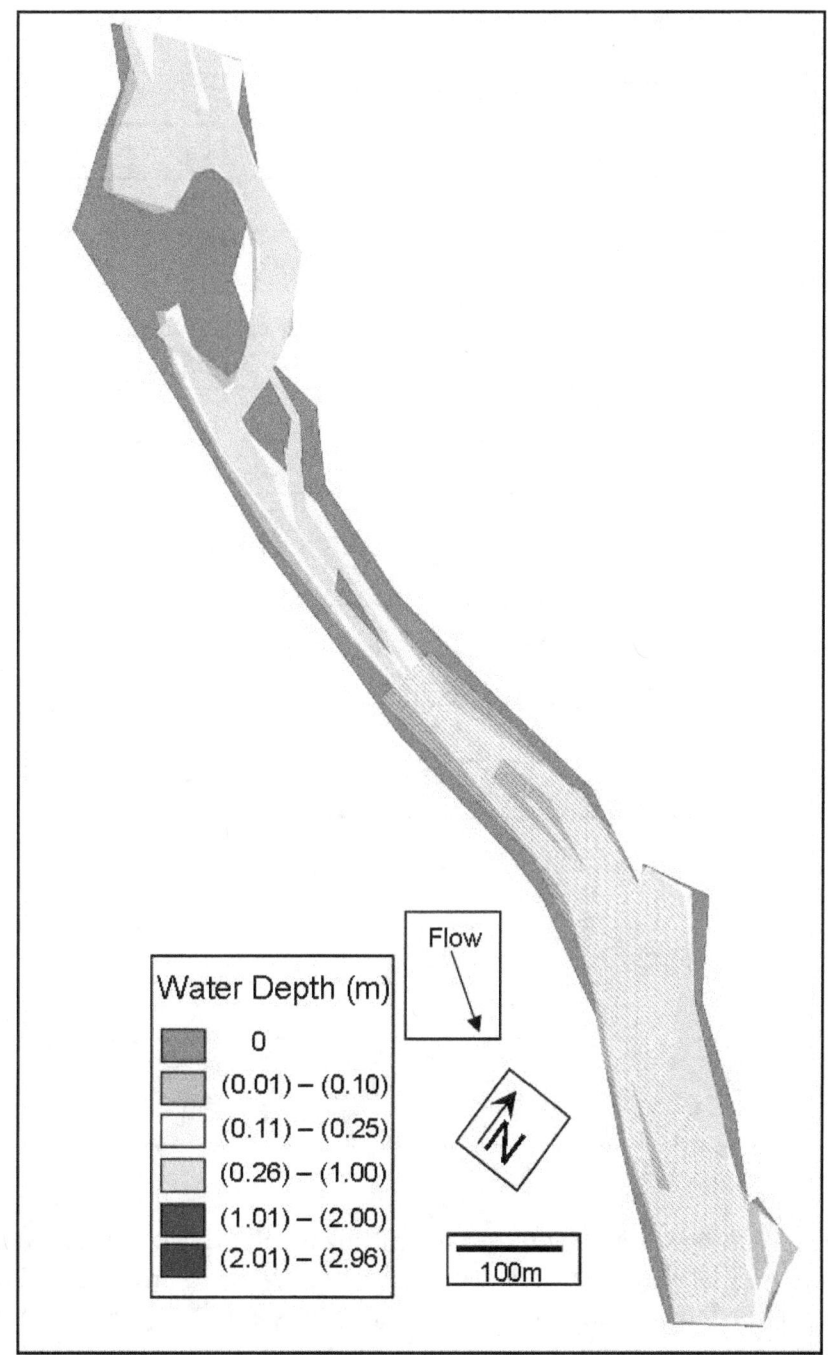

Figure 22. Map of Site 3 showing water depth (m) conditions when the fully wetted perimeter (P$_{full}$) is maintained within the site (P$_{full}$ = 77.0 m, discharge at USGS Callicoon = 26.3 cms). Grey striped area represents area known to contain *Alasmidonta heterodon* during summer 2002.

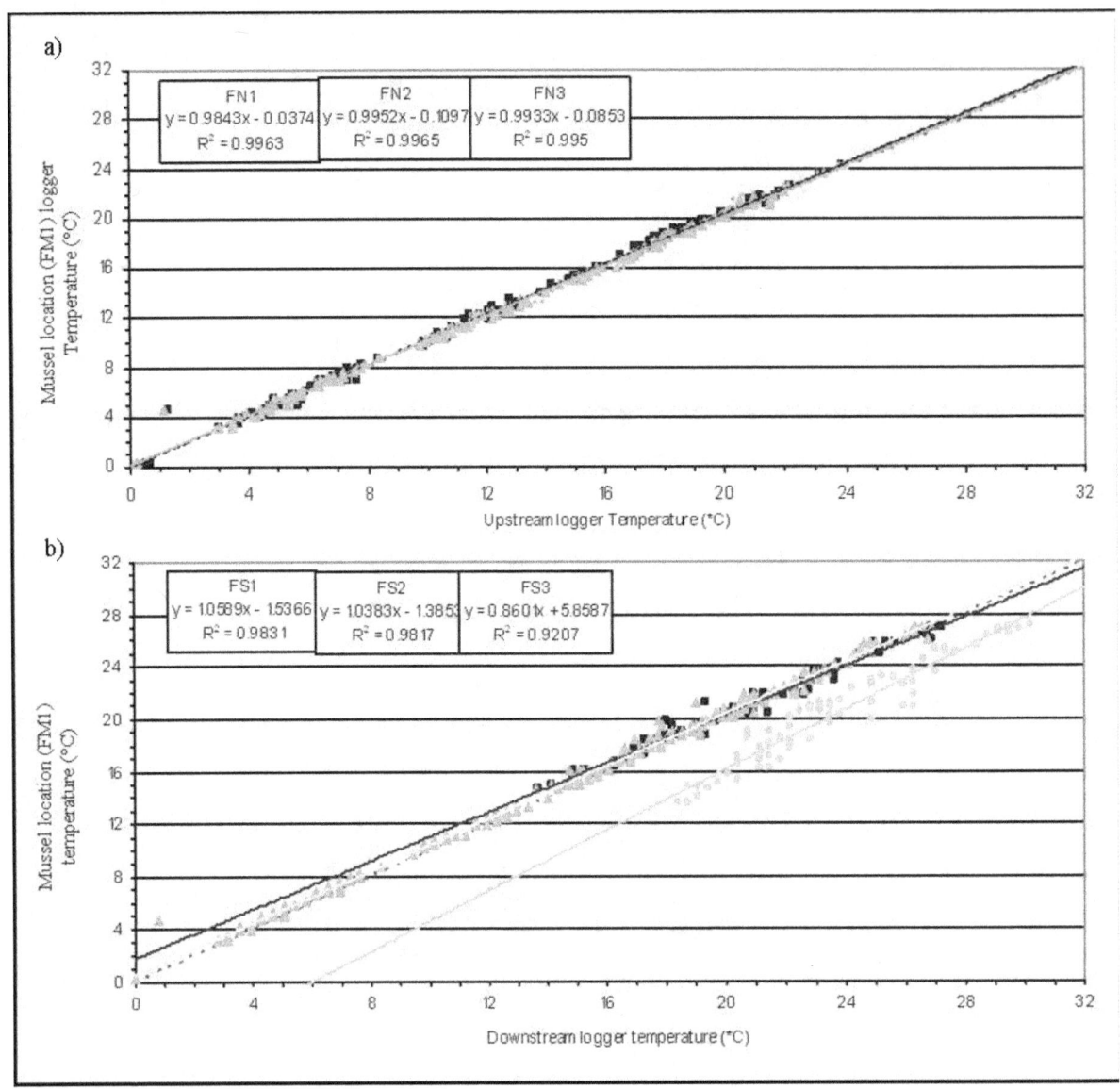

Figure 23. Within-site temperature comparisons for Site 1: a) northern data loggers (blue square data points are FN1, green triangle data points are FN2, and brown circular data points are FN3); and b) southern data loggers (blue square data points are FS1, green triangle data points are FS2, and brown circular data points are FS3). In both graphs the red dotted line represents a one to one relationship between the axes. Layout of temperature data loggers is shown in Figure 3.

There was a significant (p<0.05) F-value for the main effect of logger location on difference in temperature among loggers (Table 8). When comparing each individual within-site thermister location against the within-site mussel location, the calculated t-values for all comparisons (FM1:FN1, FM1:FN2, FM1:FN3, FM1:FS1, FM1:FS2, FM1:FS3) were significantly different (p<0.05) than zero. All were highly significant (p<0.0001) (Table 9). As a result, we rejected the null hypothesis #1 that all temperatures within the site were the same and concluded that even though there were minimal noticeable differences (e.g., Figure 23), there were statistical differences between the mussel location temperatures and all other within-site locations temperatures.

Site 2: Analyses for Site 2 showed results similar to those of Site 1. There were no major differences among temperatures recorded within the sites except at HN3, which was in the northern row of thermisters (Figure 24). The temperatures for HN3 were only slightly warmer (1°C) than the rest of the site and only during periods of generally warmer temperatures.

There was a significant (p<0.05) F-value for the main effect of thermister location on the loggers difference temperature (Table 8). When comparing each individual within-site thermister location to the within-site mussel location, the calculated t-values for three comparisons (HM1:HN2, HM1:HN3, HM1:HM2) were significantly different (p<0.05) (Table 10). As a result, we rejected the null hypothesis #1 that all temperatures within the site were the same and concluded that even though there were minimal noticeable differences (e.g., Figure 24), there were some statistical differences between the mussel location temperatures and all other within-site locations temperatures.

Site 3: While within-site temperature differences at Site 1 and Site 2 were somewhat negligible, three data logger temperatures were considerably different from the mussel location temperatures at Site 3. Temperatures at logger CN1, located in the upstream row of thermal loggers, were warmer than the mussel location within the highest temperature category (21.0–30.0°C [69.8–86°F]) (Figure 25). Temperatures at loggers CM1 and CM3, located along the same transect as the mussel location, were warmer than the mussel location for temperatures greater than 15°C (59°F). The differences in temperatures along the same thermisters row could indicate that this area of the transect provides some type of temperature refuge for *A. heterodon*.

There was a significant (p<0.05) F-value for the main effect of thermister location on the loggers difference temperature in Site 3 (Table 8). When comparing each individual within-site thermister location to the within-site mussel location, the calculated t-values for seven of the eight comparisons (CM2:CN1, CM2:CN3, CM2: CM1, CM2: CM3, CM2:CS1, CM2:CS2, CM2:CS3) were significantly different (p<0.05) from zero (Table 11). As a result, we rejected the null hypothesis #1 that all temperatures within the site were the same.

Table 8. Results from ANOVA type 3 fixed effects using time as a blocking variable for all three *Alasmidonta heterodon* sites. Significant results (P-Value < α (0.05)) are indicated in bold.

Site 1			
Effect	DF	F-Value	P-Value
Location	6	852.99	**<0.0001**
Site 2			
Effect	DF	F-Value	P-Value
Location	6	156.31	**<0.0001**
Site 3			
Effect	DF	F-Value	P-Value
Location	8	336.25	**<0.0001**

Table 9. ANOVA table for Difference of Least Squares Means comparing *Alasmidonta heterodon* thermister (FM1) against all other within-site thermisters for Site 1. Significant results (P-Value < α (0.05)) are indicated in bold.

Location 1	Location 2	DF	T-Value	P-Value
FM1	FN1	865	-5.78	**<0.0001**
FM1	FN2	865	-4.00	**0.0014**
FM1	FN3	865	-4.18	**0.0006**
FM1	FS1	865	-5.72	**<0.0001**
FM1	FS2	865	-11.62	**<0.0001**
FM1	FS3	865	50.89	**<0.0001**

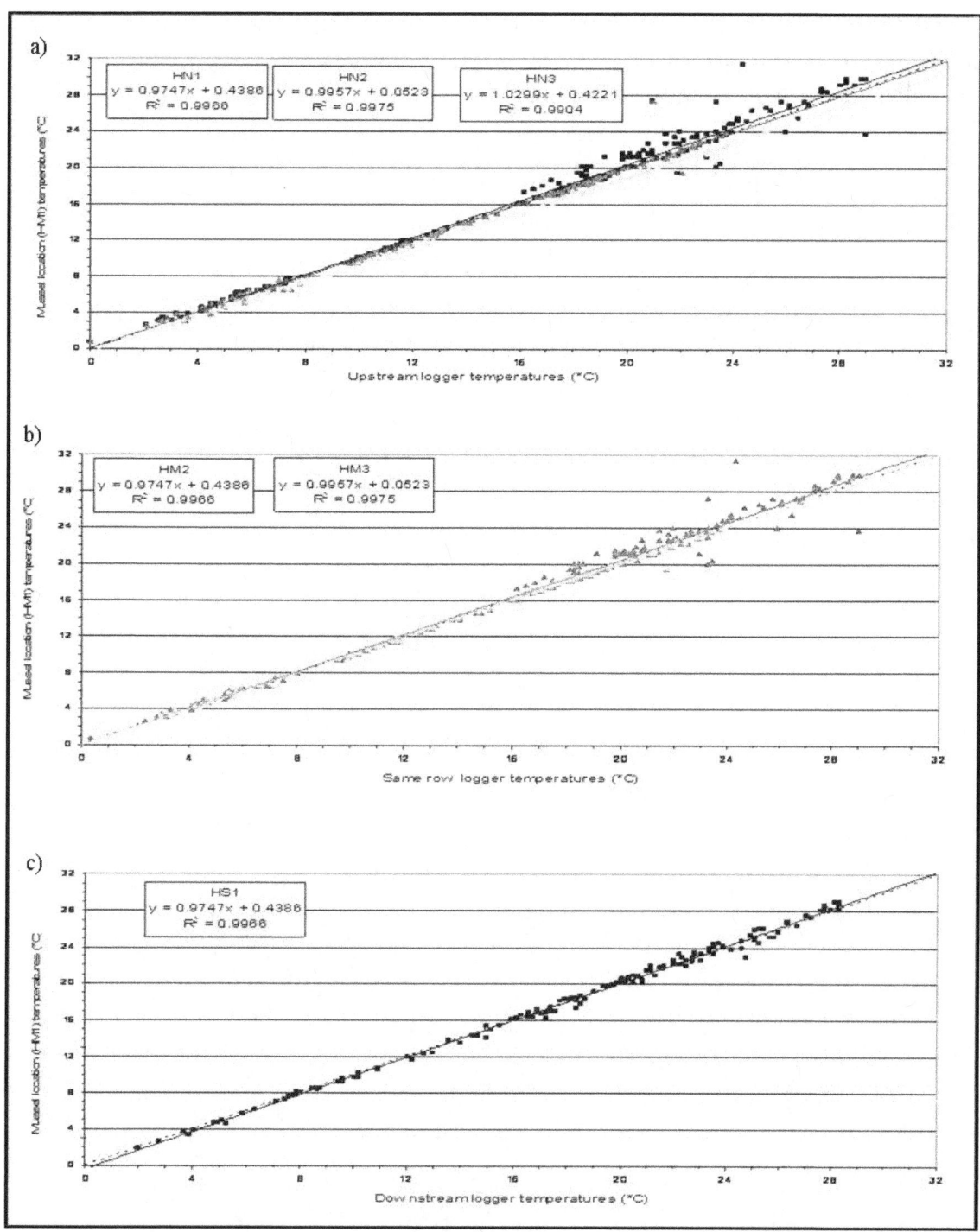

Figure 24. Within-site temperature comparisons for Site 2: a) northern data loggers (blue square data points are HN1, green triangle data points are HN2, and brown circular data points are HN3); b) middle data loggers (green triangle data points are HM2 and brown circular data points are HM3); and c) southern data loggers (blue square data points are HS1). In both graphs the red dotted line represents a one to one relationship between the axes. Layout of temperature data loggers is shown in Figure 4.

43

Table 10. ANOVA table for Difference of Least Squares Means comparing *Alasmidonta heterodon* thermister (HM1) against all other within-site thermisters for Site 2. Significant results (P-Value < α (0.05)) are indicated in bold.

Location 1	Location 2	DF	T-Value	P-Value
HM1	HN1	1011	2.59	0.1313
HM1	HN2	1011	3.89	**0.0021**
HM1	HN3	1011	23.03	**<0.0001**
HM1	HM2	1011	6.43	**<0.0001**
HM1	HM3	1011	2.81	0.0746
HM1	HS1	1011	2.33	0.2301

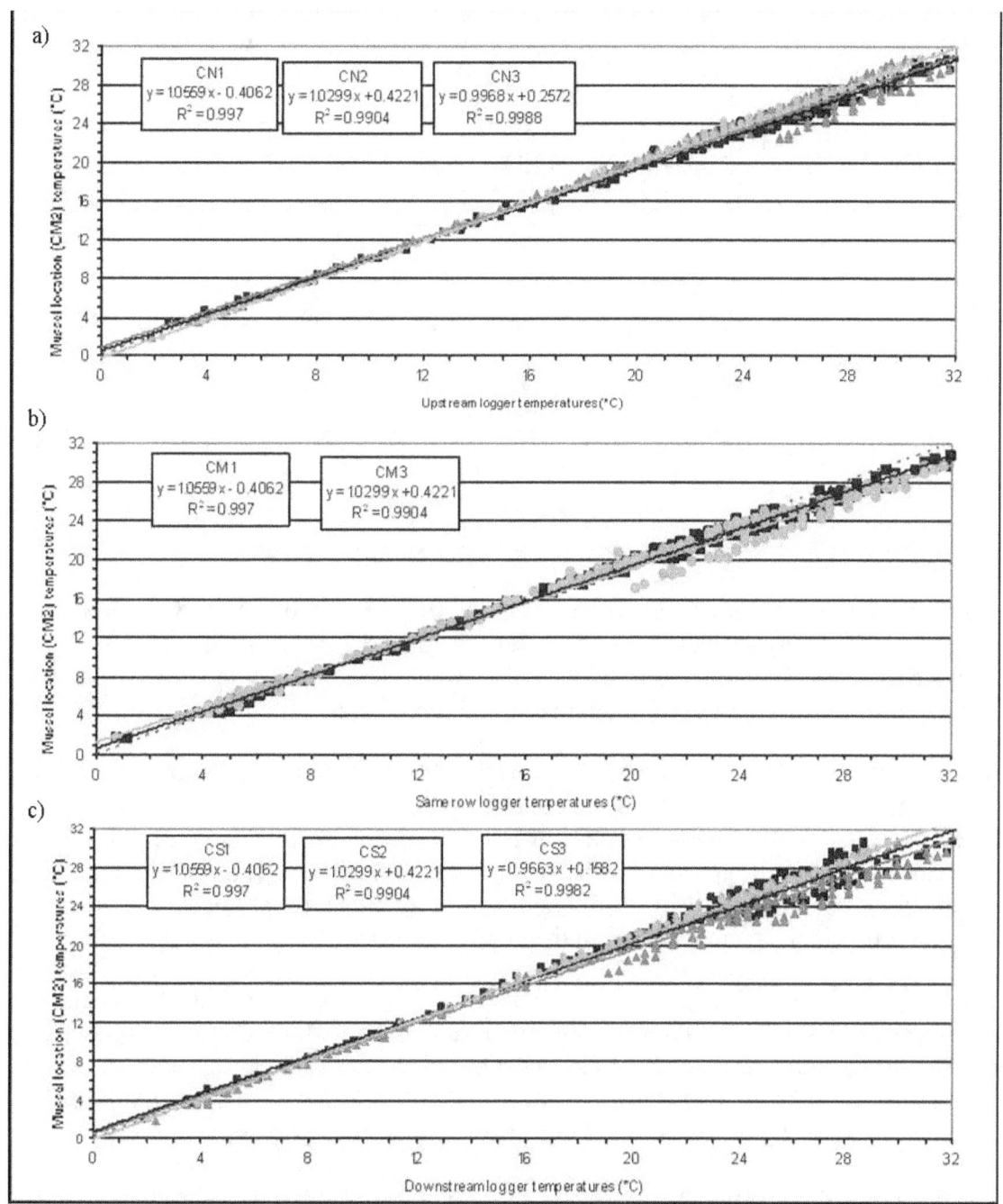

Figure 25. Within-site temperature comparisons for Site 3: a) northern data loggers (blue square data points are CN1, green triangle data points are CN2, and brown circular data points are CN3); b) middle data loggers (green triangle data points are CM2 and brown circular data points are CM3); and c) southern data loggers (blue square data points are CS1, green triangle data points are CS2, and brown circular data points are CS3). In both graphs the red dotted line represents a one to one relationship between the axes. Layout of temperature data loggers is shown in Figure 5.

Table 11. ANOVA table for Difference of Least Squares Means comparing *Alasmidonta heterodon* thermister (CM2) against all other within-site thermisters for Site 3. Significant results (P-Value < α (0.05)) are indicated in bold.

Location 1	Location 2	DF	T-Value	P-Value
CM2	CN1	1452	14.39	**<0.0001**
CM2	CN2	1452	0.88	0.9938
CM2	CN3	1452	7.18	**<0.0001**
CM2	CM1	1452	-7.19	**<0.0001**
CM2	CM3	1452	11.85	**<0.0001**
CM2	CS1	1452	-7.61	**<0.0001**
CM2	CS2	1452	4.21	**0.0009**
CM2	CS3	1452	-3.8	**0.0047**

Analysis of Site Temperatures as Compared to Surrogate Site Temperatures

Site 1: The 2005 surrogate (FMS) data formed a tightly fit linear trend (R^2=0.98) (Figure 26). Even though there was only a small range of temperature data (between 14–28°C [57.2–82.4°F]), this trend differed from the one-to-one reference line, which indicated that in 2005 the site was warmer than the surrogate measure for temperatures within the range of data.

There was a significant (p<0.05) F-value for the main effect of thermister location on difference temperature for the logger (Table 12). When comparing the *A. heterodon* thermister location against the surrogate (FMS) location, the calculated t-value for the comparison (FM1:FMS) was significantly different (p<0.05) from zero (Table 13). This significant t-value caused the null hypothesis #2 to be rejected for Site 1. We concluded the temperatures at the within-site mussel locations were different than temperatures in the other island channel.

Site 2: The 2005 surrogate (HMS) temperature data recorded in Site 2 showed a linear trend (R^2=0.85) (Figure 26). The temperatures at HMS, located in the middle of the surrogate site, were consistently warmer (~1°C [~1.8°F]) than most of the mussel locations throughout the data set. Aside from a few temperatures, the differences in temperatures were consistent through the entire range, as indicated by the linear trend line being parallel to the one-to-one reference line.

There was not a significant (p<0.05) F-value for the main effect of thermister location on difference temperature for the logger (Table 12). When comparing the *A. heterodon* thermister location (HM1) against the surrogate (HMS) location, the calculated t-value for the comparison (HM1:HMS) was not significantly different (p<0.05) from zero (Table 13). This t-value fails to reject the null hypothesis for Site 2, suggesting that there are no differences between within-site mussel location temperatures and temperatures along the opposite river bank.

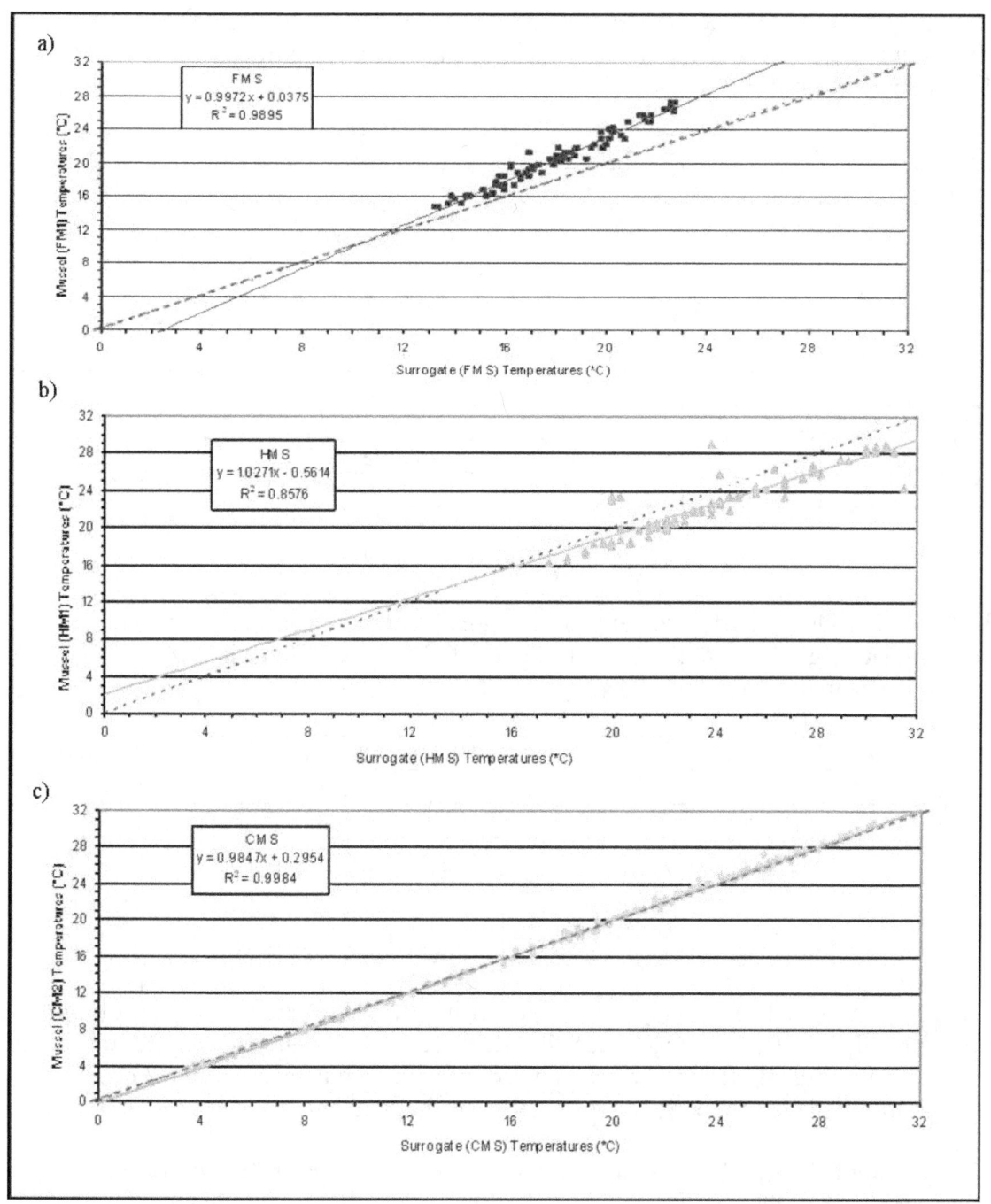

Figure 26. 2005 surrogate site temperature comparisons for: a) Site 1 (blue square data points); b) Site 2 (green triangular data points); and c) Site 3 (orange circular data points). In all graphs the red dotted line represents a one to one relationship between the axes. Layout of temperature data loggers is shown in Figures 3, 4, and 5.

Table 12. Results from ANOVA type 3 fixed effects using time as a blocking variable for all three *Alasmidonta heterodon* sites compared to surrogate locations. Significant results (P-Value < α (0.05)) are indicated in bold.

Site 1: compared to surrogate			
Effect	DF	F-Value	P-Value
Location	1	41.55	**<0.0001**

Site 2: compared to surrogate			
Effect	DF	F-Value	P-Value
Location	1	0.78	0.3777

Site 3: compared to surrogate			
Effect	DF	F-Value	P-Value
Location	1	0.12	0.7279

Table 13. ANOVA table for Difference of Least Squares Means comparing *Alasmidonta heterodon* thermisters against surrogate thermisters for all three sites. Significant results (P-Value < α (0.05)) are indicated in bold.

Location 1	Location 2	DF	T-Value	P-Value
FM1	FMS	241	6.45	**<0.0001**
HM1	HSS	154	-0.88	0.3777
CM2	CMS	164	-0.35	0.7279

Site 3: The 2005 surrogate (CMS) temperature data for in Site 3 showed a strong linear trend (R^2=0.99 [Figure 26]). There were no noticeable differences in surrogate temperatures compared to temperatures at the mussel location, which indicated the temperatures in the island channel having *A. heterodon* behaved similarly to those in the channel without *A. heterodon*.

There was not a significant ($p<0.05$) F-value for the main effect of thermister location on difference temperature for the *A. heterodon* logger (Table 12). When comparing the *A. heterodon* thermister location (CM2) against the surrogate (CMS) location, the calculated t-value for the comparison (CM2:CMS) was not significantly different ($p<0.05$) from zero (Table 13). This t-value fails to reject the null hypothesis for Site 3, indicating that there are no differences between within-site mussel location temperatures and temperatures at a similar location in the adjacent island channel along the New York bank.

Site Temperature Prediction Models

Site 1: Site 1 temperatures followed the same trend as temperatures measured at Kellams Bridge (Figure 27). Site 1 was warmer (3–4°C [5.4–7.2°F]) than both Kellams Bridge and USGS Callicoon during periods of lower temperatures (4.0–14.0°C [39.2–57.2°F]) and cooler during periods of higher temperatures (20.0–31.0°C [68.0–87.8°F]). Both established thermal gages exhibited strong linear relationships in the lower half of the temperature range (3–13°C [37.4–55.4°F]), indicated by minimum spread present in this range. The mainstem data exhibited a wider spread at temperatures greater than 20°C (68.0°F), yet temperatures at Site 1 remained notably cooler than those at both Kellams Bridge and Callicoon at these higher temperatures. In general, Kellams Bridge temperature data showed less variation with respect to Site 1 than did temperatures measured at the USGS Callicoon gage. Simple linear models did not adequately follow the trends in the temperature data for Site1, so more complex models were created for this site. Models using temperature data from Kellams Bridge (R^2=0.93) were almost equally predictive as models incorporating data from the USGS Callicoon gage (R^2=0.90). The temperature prediction model for Site 1 is:

$y = 0.0011x^3 - 0.0447x^2 + 1.1352x + 5.2587$ ($R^2 = 0.93$) (Figure 27)
   y= temperature at Site 1 (FM1) mussel location,
   x= temperature at Kellams Bridge.

Site 2: For Site 2, both the Kellams Bridge and USGS Callicoon stations showed strong linear trends which deviated very little from the one-to-one reference line (Figure 27). However, above 10°C (50°F) the Kellams Bridge location was consistently cooler than the mussel location for temperatures, while the USGS Callicoon location was consistently warmer than the mussel location in this same temperature range. The relationships between Site 2 and both Kellams Bridge and USGS Callicoon were linear, so we used a simple linear model to predict temperatures at Site 2. Models using temperature data from Kellams Bridge (R^2=0.99) were almost equally predictive as models incorporating data from the USGS Callicoon gage (R^2=0.98). The temperature prediction model for Site 2 is:

$y = 1.053\ x - 0.708$ ($R^2 = 0.99$) (Figure 27)
   y= temperature at Site 2 (HM1) mussel location,
   x= temperature at Kellams Bridge.

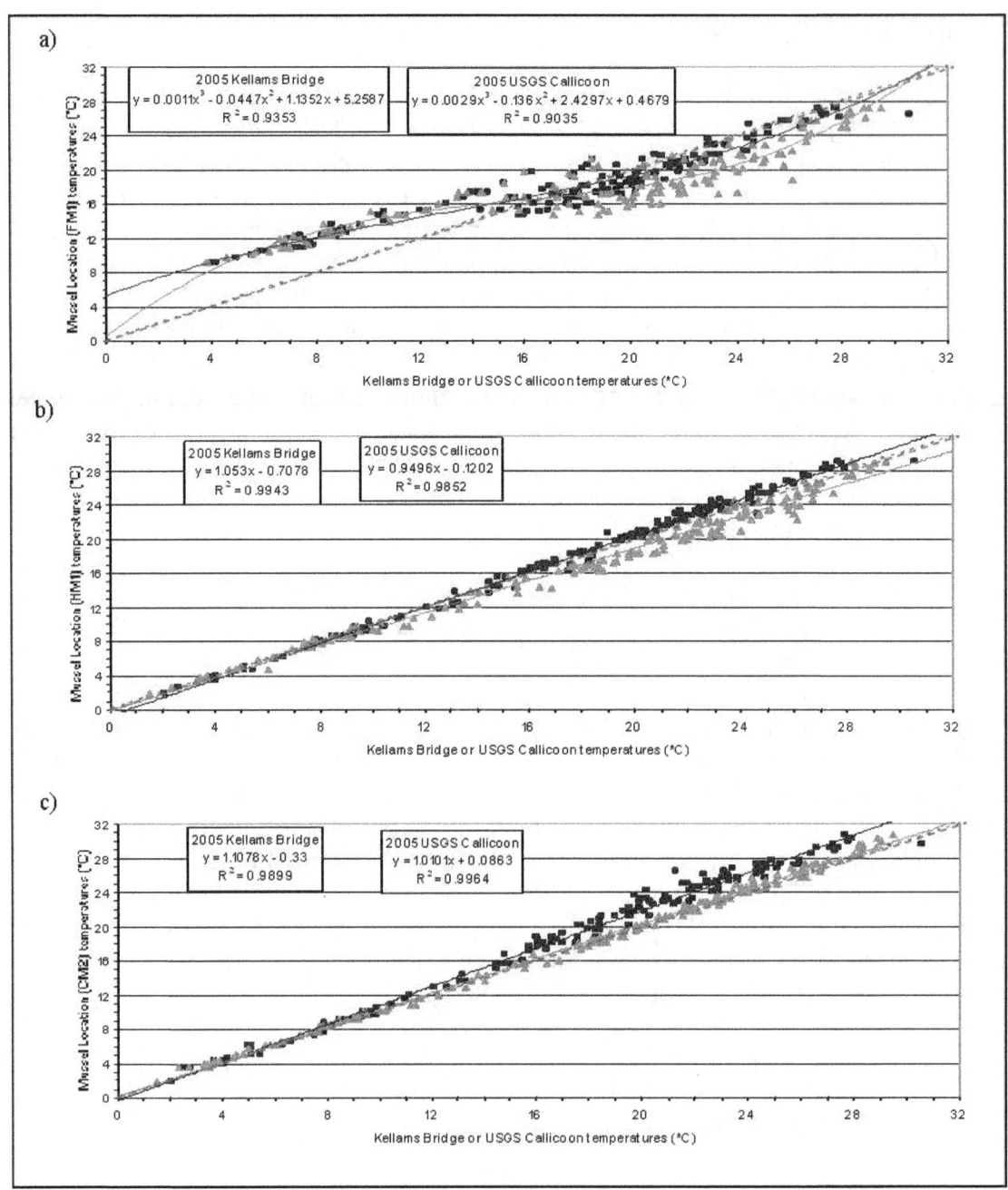

Figure 27. Comparison between *Alasmidonta heterodon* site 6pm temperatures and paired 6pm temperatures at Kellams Bridge or USGS Callicoon gage for: a) Site 1; b) Site 2; and c) Site 3. Blue square data points are 2005 Kellams Bridge data, green triangle data points are 2005 USGS Callicoon gage data, and the red dotted line represents a one-to-one relationship between the axes.

Site 3: At Site 3, both Kellams Bridge and USGS Callicoon gage temperature data showed linear trends (R^2=0.98, 0.99 [Figure 27]). When temperatures at the mussel site were below 10°C (50°F), they did not vary significantly from temperatures measured at Kellams Bridge. For temperatures warmer than 10°C (50°F), water temperatures at the mussel location were consistently warmer than those at Kellams Bridge (~1–3°C [1.8–5.4°F]). The USGS Callicoon gage temperature data showed a highly correlated linear relationship (R^2=0.99) with respect to temperatures at Site 3, indicating that there was no significant difference between Site 3 temperatures and USGS gage temperatures. We chose to use the USGS Callicoon gage in the Site 3 prediction model because of this high correlation. The Site 3 temperature prediction model is:

$$y = 1.010 \, x + 0.086 \ (R^2 = 0.99) \ \text{(Figure 27)}$$
$$y = \text{temperature at Site 3 (CM2) mussel location,}$$
$$x = \text{temperature at the USGS Callicoon gage.}$$

Relationships Between Site Temperatures and Mainstem Discharge

Site 1: Temperatures at Site 1 were as much as 5°C (9°F) warmer or 5°C (9°F) colder than Kellams Bridge temperatures (Figure 28). In the lowest temperature category (0–7.99°C [32.0–46.4°F]) deviation values were consistently between 0–5.0°C (0.0–9.0°F), indicating that site temperatures were slightly warmer than those at Kellams Bridge when discharge at the Callicoon gage was above 450 cms (15,891.6 cfs). This relatively high discharge rate could conceivably introduce a significant quantity of water from the mainstem into the mussel site, thereby reducing the differences in temperatures between mussel sites and those at Kellams Bridge on the mainstem. Many of the temperature observations in the middle (8–21.99°C [46.4–71.6°F]) and warm (22+°C [71.6+°F]) temperature ranges were between 0–2°C (0.0–3.6°F) cooler than the mainstem, suggesting a slight possibility that Site 1 could serve as a thermal refuge when water temperatures are generally high. When Kellams Bridge temperatures were above 24°C (75.2°F) and the USGS Callicoon gage discharge was below 30 cms (1,059.4 cfs), Site 1 was always colder (0.02–4.23°C [0.04–7.6°F]). The most notable difference between mainstem and Site 1 temperatures was at the Kellams Bridge at an extreme warm temperature (30.6°C [87.1°F]), which occurred at a discharge rate of ~16 cms (565 cfs) when Site 1 was noticeable colder (26.4°C [79.5°F]).

Site 2: Site 2 exhibited less variability deviation from gage temperatures in all three temperature categories (±2°C [±3.6°F {Figure 29}]). This was observed consistently at all discharge rates recorded during the course of this study, indicating that discharge has little effect on the deviation of site temperatures from river temperatures. This is likely because no physical barriers exist between Site 2 and the mainstem that would isolate that site from the effects of mainstem flows and corresponding temperatures. However, it was observed that extreme high temperatures in Site 2 were consistently warmer than those at Kellams Bridge and only occurred when USGS Callicoon discharge values were below 150 cms (5,297 cfs). In particular, when Kellams Bridge was warmer than 24°C (75.2°F) and the USGS Callicoon gage discharge was below 30 cms (1,059 cfs), Site 2 was always warmer (0.12–1.42°C [0.22–2.56°F]). The maximum temperatures at Kellams Bridge (27.8–27.9°C [82.0–82.2°F) occurred during low discharge (less than 20 cms [706.3 cfs]) and resulted in Site 2 being 1°C (1.8°F) warmer.

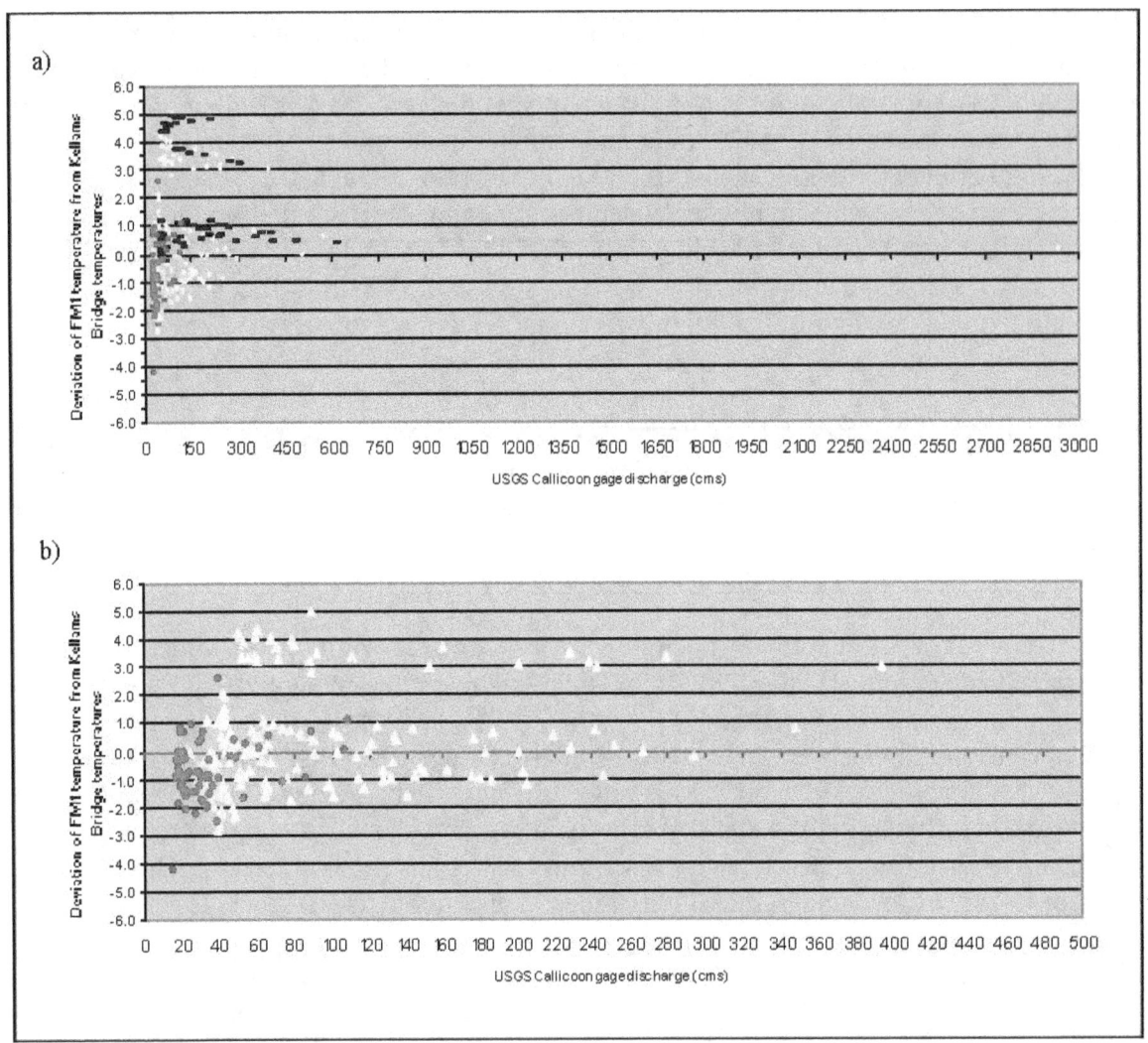

Figure 28. Site 1 temperature deviations from Kellams Bridge temperature compared to discharge rates (cms) at the USGS Callicoon gage. Plot "a" features the entire data range while plot "b" features a low flow (cms) close-up. Blue data points represent temperatures between 0.0 – 7.99°C, yellow data points represent temperatures between 8.0 – 20.99°C, and red data points represent temperatures between 21.0 – 32.0°C.

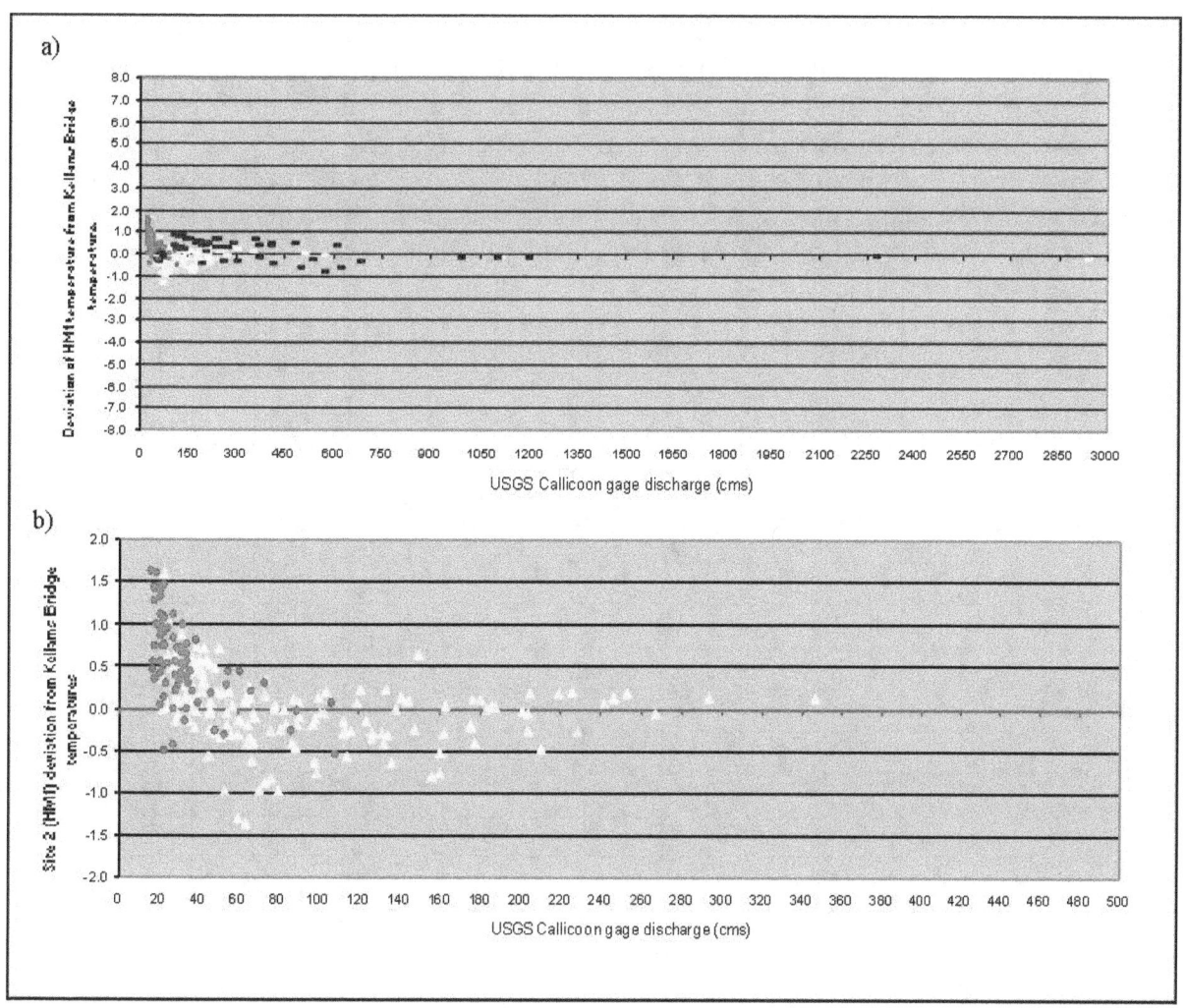

Figure 29. Site 2 temperature deviations from Kellams Bridge temperatures compared to discharge rates (cms) at the USGS Callicoon gage. Plot "a" features the entire data range while plot "b" features a low flow (cms) close-up. Blue data points represent temperatures between 0.0–7.99°C, yellow data points represent temperatures between 8.0–20.99°C, and red data points represent temperatures between 21.0–32.0°C.

Site 3: Temperatures were consistently warmer at Site 3 than they were at the USGS Callicoon gage, particularly during periods of low flow (~1°C [~1.8°F]) and higher overall temperatures (0–2°C [0.0–3.6°F {Figure 30}]). Site 3 was consistently very similar to the USGS Callicoon gage temperature in the middle temperature range (8.0–20.99°C [46.4–69.8°F]). When the USGS Callicoon gage temperatures were warmer than 24°C (75.2°F) during discharge levels below 30 cms (1,059.4 cfs), Site 3 was generally warmer than the mainstem. In particular, Site 3 was warmer by 0.93–1.15°C (1.7–2.1°F) when the highest temperatures (29.0–29.5°C [84.2–85.1°F]) were observed at the USGS Callicoon gage discharge levels below 20 cms (706.3 cfs).

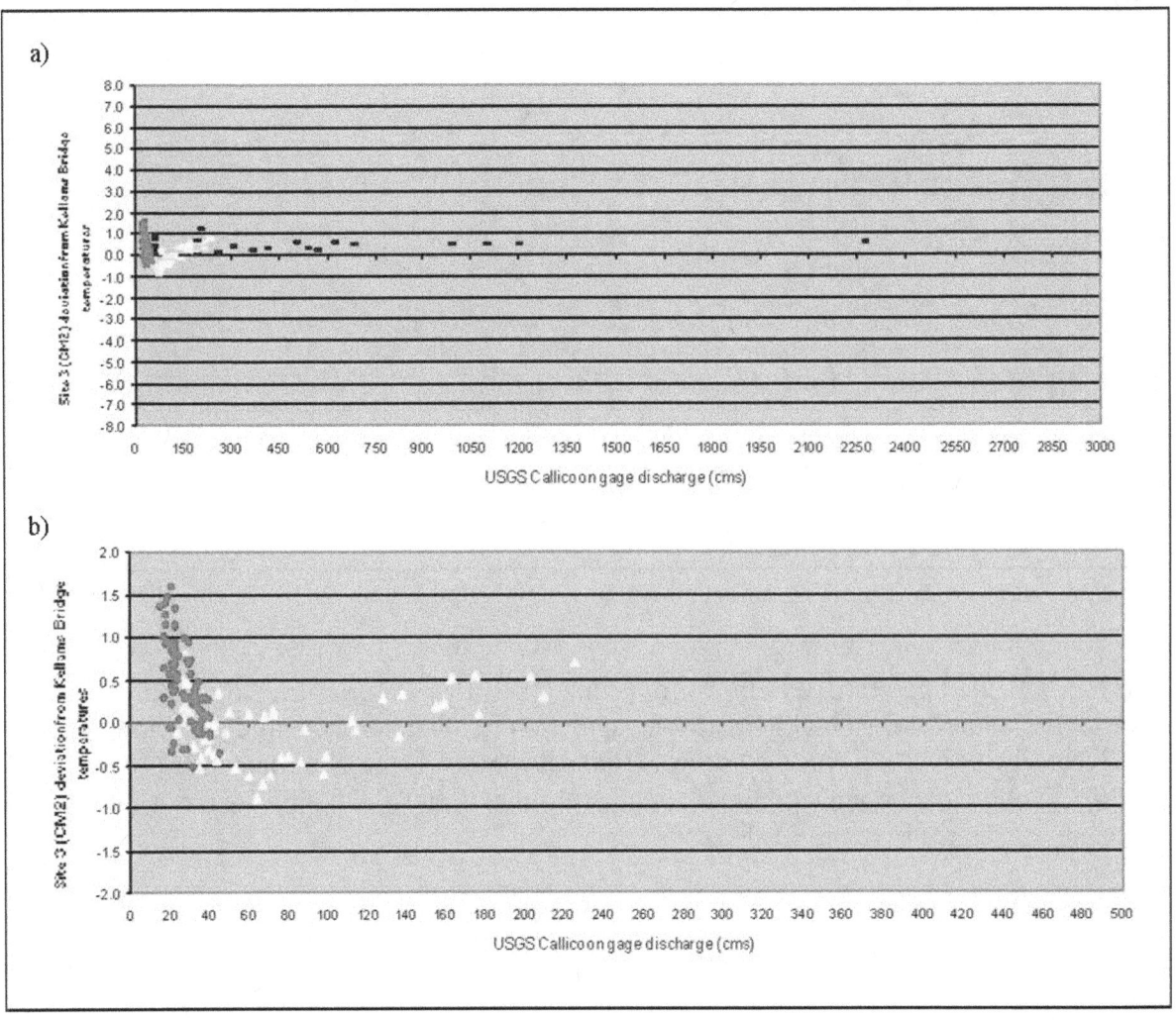

Figure 30. Site 3 temperature deviations from the USGS Callicoon gage temperature compared to discharge rates (cms) at the USGS Callicoon gage. Plot "a" features the entire data range while plot "b" features a low flow (cms) close-up. Blue data points represent temperatures between 0.0–7.99°C, yellow data points represent temperatures between 8.0–20.99°C, and red data points represent temperatures between 21.0–32.0°C.

Discussion

Evaluation of Discharge Prediction Model Method

Rating data were developed for both the full and partial river at Site 2, allowing a comparison between the calculated full river discharge at Site 2 and the discharge at the USGS Callicoon gage. Calculated discharge values were similar to the USGS Callicoon discharge values, demonstrating that the technique used to calculate the site discharge was sufficiently accurate to measure the amount of flow.

As we expected, for a majority of the Site 2 discharge levels (in the range 14–40 cms [494.4–1,412.6 cfs]), the calculated discharge followed a close one-to-one relationship with USGS Callicoon discharge data (Figure 31). A total of 109 full river discharge values for Site 2 were compared to USGS Callicoon gage discharge values, and full river values ranged between 14.8–60.0 cms (522.7–2,118.9 cfs) while USGS Callicoon discharge values ranged between 20.5–67.2 cms (724.0–2,373.1 cfs). At higher discharge rates at Site 2 (40.0–60.0 cms [1,412.6–2,118.9 cfs]), the discharge values at the USGS Callicoon gage were consistently higher (3–7 cms [105.9–247.2 cfs]) than the calculated full river discharge values at the site. This discrepancy is likely due to the linear rating curve fit to the full river data, which was appropriate for the low flow data (<45 cms [1,589 cfs]) but is not expected to be accurate for higher discharge values outside the range of our rating data. As a result, at high flows (>45 cms [1,589 cfs]) the linear rating curve for Site 2 would underestimate the discharge value, thereby accounting for the discrepancy in the higher flow range. Nevertheless, a majority of the calculated full river discharge values show the same flow at Site 2 as at the USGS gage, suggesting that the technique used provided comparable accuracy to the USGS technique and should be sufficient to determine the discharge levels at the other *A. heterodon* sites.

Implications of Flow Targets on Site Temperature

One intended outcome of this study was to identify a target discharge value at the USGS Callicoon gage (or upstream gage) that would be sufficient to keep water in the three *A. heterodon* sites to avoid potential occlusion leading to unfavorably low flows or high water temperatures. However, results from the temperature analysis indicate that Site 2 and Site 3 temperatures differ only slightly (1–2°C [1.8–3.6°F) from mainstem temperatures (Figure 29 for Site 2, Figure 30 for Site 3). This result has several possible implications. First, the extreme temperatures necessary to determine whether the sites serve as thermal refugia may simply not have occurred. Alternatively, the sites may have operated as refugia by buffering what might otherwise have been larger increases in temperature than were observed. Finally, it is unknown what amount of thermal buffering may be important to *A. heterodon*. Better data on physiological tolerances of *A. heterodon* are needed. Regardless, it was apparent that there appeared to be some warming at the *A. heterodon* sites during warm flows at discharges below 32 cms (1,130 cfs) and 27 cms (953.5 cfs) for Site 2 and Site 3, respectively, suggesting that this may be an initial target for observing *A. heterodon* response to river conditions. However, this initial interpretation is only based upon the 2005 data which did not show a strong meaningful difference from mainstem temperatures under the conditions experienced during this study.

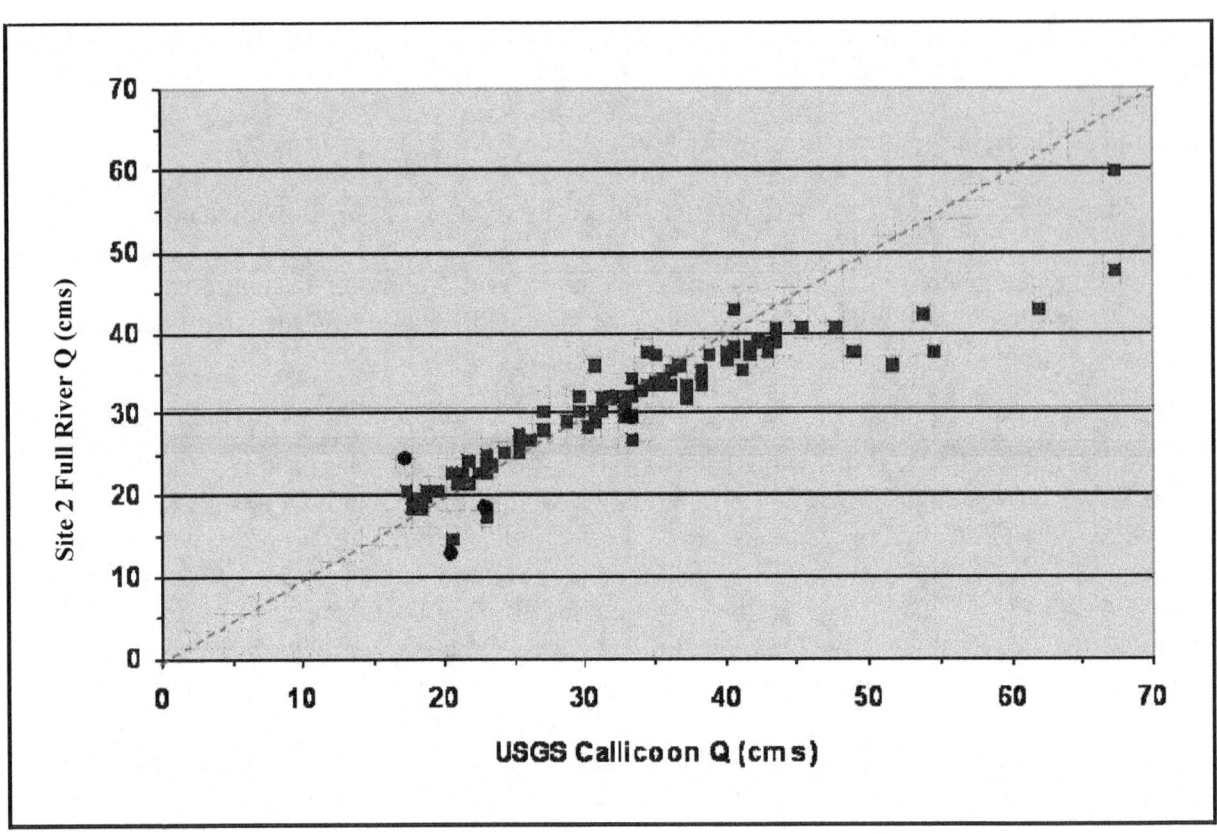

Figure 31. Calculated full river discharge (Q) at Site 2 compared to discharge (Q) at the USGS Callicoon gage. Blue square data points are calculated full river discharge (cms), and black circle data points are rating curve discharge data (cms). The red dotted line represents a one-to-one relationship between the axes.

This interpretation suggests that a flow target could be set to maintain a certain level of water within the mussel habitat in the sites, and that a separate flow target might not be necessary to prevent within-site temperatures from escalating after occlusion, as they generally follow mainstem temperatures. The small variation between within-site temperatures and mainstem temperatures indicated temperatures increase little when flow conditions drop below the point of occlusion, although this assumes that temperature increases of 1–2°C (1.8–3.6°F) are not biologically meaningful at river temperatures above 21°C (69.8°F). Unfortunately, it is unknown whether this temperature difference is physiologically significant to *A. heterodon* under high temperature. Water temperatures and low flow levels on the Delaware River during summer months appear to have complex site-specific trends, and the severity of potential threats to mussels related to thermal and hydrological stresses may vary depending upon a number of environmental variables at each location where mussels are known to occur.

In general, high temperatures coupled with low flows are known to present many potential threats to aquatic life and to freshwater mussels in particular. Our findings indicate that *A. heterodon* in the upper Delaware River may be exposed regularly to such threats—particularly at Site 3—when the mainstem river temperatures reach high levels. Low flow levels alone threaten mussels by causing the build up of waste material and by exposing mussels to increased predation in shallow areas. High water temperatures, often associated with low flow conditions, introduce additional threats. Physiological effects directly related to high water temperatures have been documented, such as breakdown in some essential enzymes within mussels (Areekijseree, Engkagul et al. 2004). Compounding factors such as changes in water chemistry may also occur, including decreases in dissolved oxygen levels that may be particularly harmful to mussels. High water temperatures have been found to cause various stress response behaviors in mussels as well, including mantle exposure through shell gaping in an effort to increase gas exchange with the surrounding environment. Increased movement, theorized to be an effort to search for favorable habitat, may also be observed (Gagnon, Golladay et al. 2004; Golladay, Gagnon et al. 2004) and has been shown to increase in frequency and intensity as water temperatures increase (Waller, Gutreuter et al. 1999).

In the Flint River, Georgia, mussel stress responses were found to be triggered when water temperatures reached 28–30°C (82.4–86°F). However, incidences of mortality were documented in this same stream in more moderate temperatures (24–26°C [75.2–78.8°F]), but were attributed to an extended period of low flows coupled with temperature fluctuations within this range (Gagnon, Golladay et al. 2004). These observed mortalities give some indication of the complicating effects even moderate temperatures have during low flow conditions, especially since thermal stress was been shown to lead to greater than 50% mortality in some mussel species (Tsuchiya 1983). This is especially troubling as conditions such as these could easily occur in the upper Delaware River, as temperatures regularly reach 24°C (75.2°F [Table 14]) or warmer during the summer and are generally coupled with periods of low flow. These negative effects were documented to occur in multiple mussel species, including *Elliptio complanata*, throughout a variety of habitat types in the Flint River; therefore, there is reason to expect that similar Atlantic slope species present in the Delaware River, including *A. heterodon*, may also be impacted by similar low flow/high temperature river conditions.

Table 14. Different USGS Callicoon gage temperatures (°C) with the corresponding number of times (#) and percentage (%) of times the daily maximum temperature was above the identified temperature. USGS Callicoon gage temperature is indicated by the value following the letter "T."

Summary Info (All)			Summary Info (1970s)			Summary Info (1980s)			Summary Info (1990s)			Summary Info (2000-2007)		
Condition	#	%	Condition	#	%	Condition	#	%	Condition	#	%	Condition	#	%
T>20	2525	25	T>20	344	25	T>20	686	26	T>20	911	26	T>20	584	23
T>21	2109	21	T>21	276	20	T>21	594	23	T>21	753	22	T>21	486	19
T>22	1720	17	T>22	216	15	T>22	502	19	T>22	604	17	T>22	398	16
T>23	1305	13	T>23	162	12	T>23	387	15	T>23	459	13	T>23	297	12
T>24	904	9	T>24	104	7	T>24	294	11	T>24	297	8	T>24	209	8
T>25	550	5	T>25	59	4	T>25	201	8	T>25	153	4	T>25	137	5
T>26	318	3	T>26	39	3	T>26	127	5	T>26	71	2	T>26	81	3
T>27	145	1	T>27	7	1	T>27	70	3	T>27	31	1	T>27	37	1
T>28	59	1	T>28	0	0	T>28	29	1	T>28	12	0	T>28	18	1
T>29	23	0	T>29	0	0	T>29	12	0	T>29	6	0	T>29	5	0
T>30	2	0	T>30	0	0	T>30	2	0	T>30	0	0	T>30	0	0

A discharge equivalent to the P_{full} condition (26.3 cms [928 cfs]) for Site 3 would likely protect *A. heterodon* at the shallowest locations it is known to occur and similar to the discharge target which would maintain thermal connectivity of the three sites. The P_{full} condition also allows for any shifting that may have occurred in the mussel population locations within the sites since discovery. Such protection may be important to mussels during key life stages.

Implications of Discharge Targets on *Alasmidonta heterodon* Life History

Freshwater mussels are unique in that they require a vertebrate host, typically a fish, in order to transform from larvae, or glochidia, into juvenile mussels (Haag and Warren 2000). Availability of fish hosts may be limited, and successful attachment of glochidia to the appropriate host is linked to presence of the fish host during periods when parent mussels release glochidia. Juvenile mussels have been shown to be sensitive to both water temperature and the oxygen tension in the water (Polhill, Dimock et al. 1996). Both water temperature and oxygen levels may become suboptimal during low flow levels, but could be mediated by maintaining P_{full} conditions.

Maintenance of constant flow levels could aid in dispersal of transformed juveniles to additional habitat within a site. By setting the discharge target (26.3 cms [928.8 cfs]) to protect the P_{full} of the sites, mussels in both the parasitic glochidia stage and early transformed juvenile stage could be protected and provided with new habitat to colonize. Such a flow target would allow not only protection of the current locations but might also aid in natural recolonization to historic habitats within the sites as well as in other areas of the river.

The shield darter (*Percina peltata*), tessellated darter (*Etheostoma olmstedi*), and slimy sculpin (*Cottus cognatus*) have been identified as fish hosts for *A. heterodon* in the Delaware River (White, Ferreri et al. 2006). Both the tessellated darter (Michaelson and Neves 1995) and the slimy sculpin (Wicklow 1999) are known to act as hosts in other drainages as well. All three of these species are benthic fishes with small home ranges (New 1966; van Snik Gray and Stauffer 1999). Increased water depth and flows over the mussels could facilitate contact with either of these host species during the glochidial life stage of *A. heterodon*. As such, an additional advantage to the P_{full} target (26.3 cms [928.8 cfs]) would be protecting habitat for these identified hosts within the three *A. heterodon* sites. While the slimy sculpin was never observed or collected within the sites, both species of darters (*P. peltata* and *E. olmstedi*) have been observed and repeatedly collected within all three sites throughout this study (White, Ferreri et al. 2006).

Etheostoma olmstedi has been observed to utilize habitat in shallow-slow water (15–27 cm [6–10.5 in], 0.12–0.20 m/sec^{-1} [0.39-0.66f/sec^{-1}]) (Bain, Finn et al. 1988; van Snik Gray and Stauffer 1999). Whereas *E. olmstedi* often employ habitat below riffles (van Snik Gray and Stauffer 1999), *Percina peltata* use habitat both at the head and in riffles within rivers and streams (New 1966). Under P_{full} conditions on the Delaware River, water depths at the mussel sites are well within the documented depth preferences for these host fish. In contrast, small shallow pools that may occur if water levels drop too low would be isolated from other habitat, and would be expected to have detrimental effects for *E. olmstedi* by reducing the availability of food and increasing the potential for predation (van Snik Gray, Kellogg et al. 2005). Deeper water depths within these sites would likely prevent habitat fragmentation for both this and other potential hosts.

Comparison of Study Findings with 2002 River Conditions

While it is reasonable to assume that *A. heterodon* generally exhibits physiological and behavioral responses similar to those of other mussel species, little research has examined specific flow and temperature needs of *A. heterodon*. In the absence of such research, field observations of this species under different temperature and flow conditions provide the only available information regarding the specific response of *A. heterodon* to certain river conditions. During a summer 2002 mussel survey, high abundances of assorted mussel species, including *A. heterodon*, were identified at all three study sites (pers. obs.). Drought during the summer of 2002 caused flow levels to be quite low (18–25 cms [635.7–882.9 cfs]) and water temperatures to be relatively high (18 days during the month of July had temperatures above 25°C [77°F]) at the USGS Callicoon gage. During the survey many mussels appeared to be stressed. In particular, we observed *A. heterodon* individuals to be significantly more stressed than other mussels such as the common *E. complanata*. Many *A. heterodon* exhibited behaviors and characteristics of thermal stress previously mentioned, such as gaping and high levels of movement. We compared results from temperature and flow models developed in this study to river conditions in 2002 in order to further evaluate whether the target discharge rates will be sufficient to protect the mussels.

When 2002 discharge and temperature data from the USGS Callicoon gage were evaluated for the time period of the 2002 mussel survey (July–August), the discharge level periodically dropped near the P_{min} flow target (15.8 cms [558 cfs]) that we identified in this study. Historic gage data along with the temperature and discharge prediction models developed in this study were used to recreate 2002 discharge and temperature conditions and wetted perimeter profiles for Site 3 for the mussel survey time period. Our predicted site conditions showed that temperatures above 25°C (77°F) occurred at the *A. heterodon* location in Site 3 when USGS Callicoon discharge rates were near the identified minimum discharge target (15.8 cms [558 cfs]). This supports the idea that the model developed in this study can be used to accurately predict conditions at Site 3, but that such a discharge target may not be sufficient to prevent adverse temperature conditions at Site 3.

While much of summer 2002 was characterized by generally high temperatures and low flows, most extreme conditions occurred during July 31–August 6. Site 3 temperatures during this period were calculated to be 23–29°C (73.4–84.2°F) and USGS Callicoon discharge rates were 20–28 cms (706.3–988.8cfs). Even though this discharge level at the USGS Callicoon gage was above the P_{min} flow target for wetted perimeter during this time period, it appears that temperatures remained quite high. Mussels at Site 3, including all the *A. heterodon*, were observed to exhibit stress responses during this time period of lower flows (20–28 cms [706.3–988.8cfs]) and high temperatures. As such, we expect that designation of a discharge target purely to protect P_{min} (15.8 cms [558 cfs]) may not adequately prevent environmental stress to mussels when temperatures are high.

This example from July and August of 2002 illustrates that water temperatures can influence the level of impact of low flow levels. Importantly, the combination of flows, ambient temperature, and water temperature all play a role. The flow levels during 2002 at the USGS Callicoon gage were not unique; throughout the past 31 years of daily USGS Callicoon gage discharge data, river conditions have dropped below the established minimum wetted perimeter flow target of this study (15.8 cms [558 cfs]) 134 times (Table 15). An evaluation of recent discharge data at Callicoon (2000–2006) shows that the P_{min} values at Site 3 (the most vulnerable of the three sites) were met 99% of the time. Therefore, the mainstem flow level rarely drops below levels that would result in wetted perimeter values less than the P_{min} for each site (Table 15). As long as this P_{min} is maintained, current *A. heterodon* sites may be protected from dewatering, although not necessarily under ideal conditions, In contrast, flow targets associated with P_{full} (26.3 cms [928.8 cfs] at the USGS Callicoon gage) and thermal stability (corresponding to 27.6 cms [974.7 cfs]) target for Site 3 are met 91% and 88% of time, indicating there still could be issues of dewatering if the population shifts, and that thermal stress may remain a threat to the existing populations.

A comparison of the flow target results of this study to the historic flow records at the USGS Callicoon gage further support the need to more closely monitor flow levels in the upper Delaware. Analyses of historic flows show that in 1985, daily flow once dropped to 8.8 cms (310.8 cfs [8/23/85]) which is well below even the P_{min} discharge level for all three sites. Low daily discharges ($Q<20$ cms [706.3 cfs]) declined during the subsequent decades (Table 15). These declines in low flow occurrence may be the consequence of a number of factors. For example, the 1990s appear to have had enough summer rainfall to sustain water levels in the river during critical time periods. Since 2000, changes to the reservoir release schedules may have limited the occurrence of low flows. In any event, periods of very low flows (<20 cms [706.3 cfs]) should be prevented in the future during summer months to protect *A. heterodon* within the three sites. Recent studies have shown that chronic prolonged moderately low water levels pose just as much threat of mortality in mussels as a single severe event (Tsuchiya 1983; Waller, Gutreuter et al. 1999; Gagnon, Golladay et al. 2004). The stressed condition of the *A. heterodon* and other mussel species during summer 2002 could indicate that the prolonged nature of this low flow/high temperature period (34 days [Table 15 for flow and Table 14 for temperature]), despite that fact that P_{min} levels were maintained, exceeded the tolerance of the mussels. Therefore, minimum flows should be set higher than the P_{min} target to minimize the effects of these conditions, particularly during the warmer summer months. As a result, it may be important to mainstem flows at or above the P_{full} (26.3 cms [928.8 cfs]). Coincidentally, this flow level is near the thermal stability threshold (27.6 cms [974.7cfs]) at which we identified small (but possibly significant) increases in site temperature at Site 2 and Site 3. Since 2000, the P_{full} flow target was maintained 91% of the time and the target flow for thermal stability was met 88% of the time (Table 15).

Table 15. Different USGS Callicoon gage discharge rates (cms) with corresponding number of days (#) during historic gage data when rate dropped below the identified rate, as well as the percentage (%) of the time period the number constituted. USGS Callicoon discharge rates are indicated by the value following the letter "Q" in the first column.

Summary Info (All)			Summary Info (1070s)			Summary Info (1980s)			Summary Info (1990s)			Summary Info (2000-2006)		
Condition	#	%	Condition	#	%	Condition	#	%	Condition	#	%	Condition	#	%
Q<40	5474	48	Q<40	701	43	Q<40	2055	56	Q<40	1839	50	Q<40	877	35
Q<38	5027	44	Q<38	647	39	Q<38	1892	52	Q<38	1703	47	Q<38	783	31
Q<36	4529	39	Q<36	602	37	Q<36	1708	47	Q<36	1539	42	Q<36	678	27
Q<34	4082	36	Q<34	547	33	Q<34	1549	42	Q<34	1381	38	Q<34	603	24
Q<32	3418	30	Q<32	467	28	Q<32	1324	36	Q<32	1138	31	Q<32	489	19
Q<30	2820	25	Q<30	388	24	Q<30	1103	30	Q<30	946	26	Q<30	383	15
Q<28	2328	20	Q<28	314	19	Q<28	933	26	Q<28	778	21	Q<28	303	12
Q<26	1850	16	Q<26	237	14	Q<26	758	21	Q<26	618	17	Q<26	237	9
Q<24	952	8	Q<24	161	10	Q<24	565	15	Q<24	458	13	Q<24	179	7
Q<22	952	8	Q<22	123	7	Q<22	399	11	Q<22	312	9	Q<22	118	5
Q<20	597	5	Q<20	91	6	Q<20	263	7	Q<20	205	6	Q<20	38	2
Q<19	446	4	Q<19	71	4	Q<19	209	6	Q<19	143	4	Q<19	23	1
Q<18	351	3	Q<18	63	4	Q<18	173	5	Q<18	100	3	Q<18	15	1
Q<17	272	2	Q<17	47	3	Q<17	141	4	Q<17	76	2	Q<17	8	0
Q<16	190	2	Q<16	39	2	Q<16	96	3	Q<16	50	1	Q<16	5	0
Q<15	133	1	Q<15	25	2	Q<15	71	2	Q<15	35	1	Q<15	2	0
Q<14	91	1	Q<14	21	1	Q<14	51	1	Q<14	18	0	Q<14	1	0
Q<13	63	1	Q<13	14	1	Q<13	34	1	Q<13	14	0	Q<13	1	0
Q<12	26	0	Q<12	2	0	Q<12	17	0	Q<12	7	0	Q<12	0	0
Q<11	15	0	Q<11	1	0	Q<11	9	0	Q<11	5	0	Q<11	0	0
Q<10	6	0	Q<10	1	0	Q<10	4	0	Q<10	1	0	Q<10	0	0
Q<9	1	0	Q<9	0	0	Q<9	1	0	Q<9	0	0	Q<9	0	0
Q<8	0	0	Q<8	0	0	Q<8	0	0	Q<8	0	0	Q<8	0	0

Conclusions

Findings from this study indicate that Site 3 is the most vulnerable of the three sites based upon discharge levels required to: 1) maintain minimal flow into the site, 2) maintain the minimal wetted perimeter, and 3) maintain the fully wetted perimeter (Table 16). This study also indicated that if Site 3 is protected the other two sites would likely remain protected, as indicated by the lower USGS Callicoon gage discharge levels required to maintain similar conditions in Site 1 and Site 2. Depending upon how management objectives are related to *A. heterodon* in the Delaware River, one of these flow targets may be justified. We conclude by outlining how our flow targets could fit into some possible management objectives.

Occlusions occur when discharge at the USGS Callicoon gage is at 12.8 cms (452 cfs). A discharge of 15.8 cms (558 cfs) at the USGS Callicoon gage is required to maintain minimal wetted perimeter (P_{min}) which provides a water refuge within the site in areas where the *A. heterodon* were originally found. The stressed condition of *A. heterodon* within Site 3 during 2002 under low flow conditions (20.8 cms [734.5 cfs]) and warm water temperatures (27.5°C [81.5°F]) at the USGS Callicoon gage, suggests that this P_{min} flow target may not be sufficient to protect the *A. heterodon* when flow levels are low and water temperatures are high. A discharge of 26.3 cms (928.8 cfs) at the USGS Callicoon gage is required to maintain the fully wetted perimeter (P_{full}) which allows for any shifting in mussel locations within the site that may have occurred since the 2002 Lellis survey. A discharge above 30 cms (1,059 cfs) for Site 2 and 27.6 cms (974.7 cfs) for Site 3 is required to maintain site within two degrees of mainstem temperatures. However, it is unknown whether this temperature difference is physiologically significant to *A. heterodon* under high temperature, low flow conditions.

One intended outcome of this study was to identify a discharge value at the USGS Callicoon gage (or an upstream gage) that would be sufficient to protect the three *A. heterodon* sites from potential occlusion related to unfavorably low flow high water temperatures. However, results from the temperature analysis indicate that Site 2 and Site 3 temperatures differ only slightly (1–2°C [1.8–3.6°F]) from mainstem temperatures. This result has several potential implications. First, the extreme temperatures necessary to evaluate the sites as refugia simply did not occur. Alternatively, the sites may have operated as refugia by buffering what might otherwise have been larger increases in temperature than were observed. There is evidence in the literature that some mussel species do become subject to temperature stress above 24°C (75.2°F), so we cannot discount the possibility that temperature increases observed at the sites at low/warm flows are not significant for *A. heterodon*. Further physiological and hydrological studies are likely needed to better assess an optimal flow rate to maintain site thermal conditions.

Table 16. Calculated USGS gage discharge levels corresponding to the zero discharge stage height conditions within the sites, the minimum wetted perimeter (P_{min}) in each study site, the fully wetted perimeter (P_{full}) in each site, and the thermal stability (site temperature within 1°C of mainstem temperature): a) cms (R^2 value), and b) cfs (R^2 value).

a)

Site	Zero Discharge (cms)	Minimally Wetted P_{min} (cms)	Fully Wetted P_{full} (cms)	Thermal Stability (cms)
Site 1	6.4 (R^2=0.85)	9.7 (R^2=0.85)	13.9 (R^2=0.85)	--
Site 2	0.0 (R^2=0.96)	3.4 (R^2=0.96)	14.0 (R^2=0.96)	30.0 (R^2=0.96)
Site 3	12.8 (R^2=0.96)	15.8 (R^2=0.96)	26.3 (R^2=0.96)	27.6 (R^2=0.96)

b)

Site	Zero Discharge (cfs)	Minimally Wetted P_{min} (cfs)	Fully Wetted P_{full} (cfs)	Thermal Stability (cfs)
Site 1	226 (R^2=0.85)	342 (R^2=0.85)	491 (R^2=0.85)	--
Site 2	0.0 (R^2=0.96)	120 (R^2=0.96)	494 (R^2=0.96)	1059 (R^2=0.96)
Site 3	452 (R^2=0.96)	558 (R^2=0.96)	928 (R^2=0.96)	974 (R^2=0.96)

Literature Cited

Areekijseree, M., A. Engkagul, et al. 2004. Temperature and pH characteristics of amylase and proteinase of adult freshwater pearl mussel, Hyriopsis (Hyriopsis) bialatus Simpson 1900. Aquaculture 234(1–4):575–587.

Bain, M. B., J. T. Finn, et al. 1988. Streamflow regulation and fish community structure. Ecology 69(2):382–392.

Bovee, K. D., T. J. Waddle, et al. 2007. A decision support framework for water management in the upper Delaware River. U. S. Geological Survey. Open-File Report 2007-1172. 122 pp.

Fenton, J. D., and R. J. Keller. 2001. The calculation of streamflow from measurements of stage. Cooperative Research Centre for Catchment Hydrology. 75 pp.

Gagnon, P. M., S. W. Golladay, et al. 2004. Drought responses of freshwater mussels (Unionidae) in coastal plain tributaries of the Flint River basin, Georgia. Journal of Freshwater Ecology 19(4):667–679.

Golladay, S. W., P. Gagnon, et al. 2004. Response of freshwater mussel assemblages (Bivalvia: Unionidae) to a record drought in the Gulf Coastal Plain of southwestern Georgia. Journal of the North American Benthological Society 23(3):494–506.

Haag, W. R., and M. L. Warren. 2000. Effects of light and presence of fish on lure display and larval release behaviours in two species of freshwater mussels. Animal Behaviour 60:879–886.

Lellis, W. A. 2001. Freshwater mussel survey of the Upper Delaware Scenic and Recreational River: Qualitative Survey 2000. U.S. Geological Survey - Northern Appalachian Research Laboratory. Wellsboro, PA. 56 pp.

Michaelson, D. L., and R. J. Neves. 1995. Life history and habitat of the endangered dwarf wedgemussel *Alasmidonta heterdon* (Bilvalvia, Unionidae). Journal of the North American Benthological Society 14(2):324–340.

Morales, Y., L. J. Weber, et al. 2006. Effects of substrate and hydrodynamic conditions on the formation of mussel beds in a large river. Journal of the North American Benthological Society 25(3):664–676.

New, J. G. 1966. Reproductive behavior of the shield darter, *Percina peltata peltata*, in New York. Copeia 1966(1):20–28.

Polhill, J. B., V. Dimock, et al. 1996. Effects of temperature and pO(2) on the heart rate of juvenile and adult freshwater mussels (Bivalvia: Unionidae). Comparative Biochemistry and Physiology a-Physiology 114(2):135–141.

Serio, J. 2002. The finest in the East: the tailwater trout fishery of the upper Delaware River. American Fisheries Society 132nd Annual Meeting. Baltimore, MD. American Fisheries Society.

Tsuchiya, M. 1983. Mass mortality in a population of the mussel *Mytilus edulis* caused by high temperature on rocky shores. The Journal of Experimental Marine Biology and Ecology 66:101–111.

USFWS. 1993. Dwarf Wedge Mussel (*Alasmidonta heterodon*) Recovery Plan, U.S. Fish and Wildlife Services: 51.

van Snik Gray, E., K. A. Kellogg, et al. 2005. Habitat shift of a native darter *Etheostoma olmstedi* (Teleostei: Percidae) in sympatry with a non-native darter Etheostoma zonale. American Midland Naturalist 154(1):166–177.

van Snik Gray, E., and J. R. Stauffer. 1999. Comparative microhabitat use of ecologically similar benthic fishes. Environmental Biology of Fishes 56(4):443–453.

Vandermeer, J., B. Hoffman, et al. 2001. Effect of habitat fragmentation on gypsy moth (*Lymantria dispar* L.) dispersal: The quality of the matrix. American Midland Naturalist 145(1):188–193.

Waller, D. L., S. Gutreuter, et al. 1999. Behavioral responses to disturbance in freshwater mussels with implications for conservation and management. Journal of the North American Benthological Society 18(3):381–390.

White, B. S., C. P. Ferreri, et al. 2006. Evaluation of potential fish hosts for the endangered dwarf wedgemussel (*Alasmidonta heterodon*) in the Delaware River basin. Annual meeting of American Fisheries Society. Lake Placid, NY.

Wicklow, B. J. 1999. Life history of the endangered dwarf wedgemussel, *Alasmidonta heterodon*: Glochidial release, phenology, mantle display behavior and anadromous fish host relationship. Program Guide and Abstract of the First Symposium of the Freshwater Mollusk Conservation Society. Chattanooga, TN.

As the nation's primary conservation agency, the Department of the Interior has responsibility for most of our nationally owned public land and natural resources. This includes fostering sound use of our land and water resources; protecting our fish, wildlife, and biological diversity; preserving the environmental and cultural values of our national parks and historical places; and providing for the enjoyment of life through outdoor recreation. The department assesses our energy and mineral resources and works to ensure that their development is in the best interests of all our people by encouraging stewardship and citizen participation in their care. The department also has a major responsibility for American Indian reservation communities and for people who live in island territories under U.S. administration.

NPS D-068A July 2008